Aristophanes' The Birds

THE FOCUS CLASSICAL LIBRARY
Series Editors • James Clauss and Stephen Esposito

Aristophanes' The Birds

Translated with
Introduction and Notes

Jeffrey Henderson

Boston University

focus an imprint of
Hackett Publishing Company, Inc.
Indianapolis/Cambridge

Previously published by Focus Publishing / R. Pullins Company

Focus an imprint of
Hackett Publishing Company, Inc.
P.O. Box 44937
Indianapolis, Indiana 46244-0937

www.hackettpublishing.com

For information regarding performance rights,
please email us at Permissions@hackettpublishing.com

Cover image copyright © istockphoto / Kary Fisher

ISBN 13: 978-0-941051-87-3

Contents

INTRODUCTION

Aristophanes and Old Comedy

Aristophanes of Athens, the earliest comic playwright from whom whole works survive, was judged in antiquity to be the foremost poet of Old Attic Comedy, a theatrical genre of which he was one of the last practitioners and of which his eleven surviving plays are our only complete examples. His plays are valued principally for the exuberance of their wit and fantasy, for the purity and elegance of their language, and for the light they throw on the domestic and political life of Athens in an important era of its history. Legend has it that when the Syracusan tyrant Dionysius wanted to inform himself about "the republic of the Athenians," Plato sent him the plays of Aristophanes.

Little is known about Aristophanes' life apart from his theatrical career. He was born *ca.* 447/6, the son of one Philippus of the urban deme Cydathenaeum and the tribe Pandionis, and he died probably between 386 and 380. By his twenties his hair had thinned or receded enough that his rivals could call him bald. He seems to have had land-holdings on, or some other connection with, the island of Aegina, a connection that detractors and enemies exploited early in his career in an attempt to call his Athenian citizenship into question. In the 420s he was twice prosecuted by a fellow demesman, the popular politician Cleon, for the political impropriety of two of his plays (*Babylonians* of 426 and *Knights* of 424), but neither time was he convicted. Early in the fourth century he represented his tribe in the prestigious government position of Councillor. Four comic poets of the fourth century, Araros, Philetaerus, Philippus and Nicostratus, are reputed in ancient sources to be his sons.

In the dialogue *Symposium* Plato portrays Aristophanes as being at home among the social and intellectual elite of Athens. Although the historical truth of Plato's portrayal is uncertain, Aristophanes' plays do generally espouse the social, moral and political sentiments of contemporary upper-class conservatives: nostalgia for the good old days of the early democracy,

1

which defeated the Persians and built the empire; dismay at the decadence, corruption and political divisiveness of his own day; hostility toward the new breed of populist leaders who emerged after the death of the aristocratic Perikles in 429; impatience with the leadership and slow progress of the Peloponnesian War (431-404), particularly when it threatened the interests of the landowning classes; and unhappiness about many of the artistic and intellectual trends of his own day, especially those he regarded as harming the high art of drama. There is no question that Aristophanes' comic expression of such views reflected, and to a degree shaped, community opinion, and that comedy could occasionally have a distinct social and political impact. But the fact that Aristophanes emerged politically and artistically unscathed from the war, from two oligarchic revolutions (411 and 404), and from two democratic restorations (411 and 403) suggests that on the whole his role in Athenian politics was more satirical, moral(istic) and poetical than practical; and the perennial popularity of his plays would seem to indicate that the sentiments they express were broadly shared at least among the theatrical public.

The period of Old Comedy at Athens began in 486 BC, when comedy first became part of the festival of the Greater Dionysia; by convention it ended in 388 BC, when Aristophanes produced his last play. During this period some 600 comedies were produced. We know the titles of some fifty comic poets and the titles of some 300 plays. We have eleven complete plays by Aristophanes, the first one (*Acharnians*) dating from 425, and several thousand fragments of other plays by Aristophanes and other poets, most of them only a line or so long and very few deriving from plays written before 440.

The principal occasions for the production of comedies were the Greater Dionysia, held in late March or early April, and (from 440) the Lenaea, held in late January or early February. These were national festivals honoring the wine-god Dionysus, whose cult from very early times had included mimetic features. The theatrical productions that were the highlight of the festivals were competitions in which poets, dancers, actors, producers and musicians competed for prizes that were awarded by judges at the close of the festival. The Greater Dionysia was held in the Theater of Dionysus on the south slope of the Acropolis, which accommodated some 17,000 spectators, including both Athenian and foreign visitors. The Lenaea, which only Athenians attended, was held elsewhere in the city (we do not know where). By the fourth century the Lenaea was held in the Theater of Dionysus also, but it is unclear when the relocation occurred.

At these festivals comedy shared the theater with tragedy and satyr-drama, genres that had been produced at the Greater Dionysia since the sixth century. The first "city" contest in tragedy is dated to 534, when the victorious actor-poet was Thespis (from whose name actors are still called thespians). But it is not certain that Thespis' contest was held at the Greater Dionysia, and in any case this festival seems to have experienced major changes after the overthrow of the tyranny and the establishment of democracy, that is, after the reforms of Cleisthenes in 508. Tragedy dramatized stories from heroic myth, emphasizing dire personal and social events that had befallen hero(in)es and their families in the distant past, and mostly in places other than Athens. By convention, the poetry and music of tragedy were highly stylized and archaic. Satyr-drama, which was composed by the same poets who wrote tragedy, had similar conventions, except that the heroic stories were treated in a humorous fashion and the chorus was composed of satyrs: mischievous followers of Dionysus who were part human and part animal.

Comedy, by contrast, had different conventions of performance (see Production, below) and was less restricted by conventions of language, music and subject. That is probably why the composers and performers of tragedy and satyr-drama were never the same ones who composed and performed comedy. The language of comedy was basically colloquial, though it often parodies the conventions of other (particularly tragic) poetry, and was free to include indecent, even obscene material. The music and dancing, too, tended to reflect popular styles. The favorite subjects of comedy were free-form mythological burlesque; domestic situations featuring everyday character types; and political satire portraying people and events of current interest in the public life of the Athenians. Our eleven surviving comedies all fall into this last category. Mythological and domestic comedy continued to flourish after the Old Comic period, but political comedy seems to have died out: a casualty not merely of changing theatrical tastes but also of the social and political changes that followed the Athenians' loss of the Peloponnesian War, and with it their empire, in 404. To understand the significance of political comedy, we must look first at the political system of which it was an organic feature: the phase of radical democracy inaugurated by the reforms of Ephialtes in 462/1 and lasting until the end of the century.

Democracy means "rule of the demos" (sovereign people). In fifth-century Athens democracy was radical in that the sovereignty of the demos was more absolute than in any other society before or since. The demos consisted of all citizen males at least eighteen years of age. All decisions affecting the governance and welfare of the state were made by the direct and unappealable vote of the demos. The state was managed by members of the demos at least thirty years of age, who were chosen by lot from a list of eligible citizens and who held office in periods ranging from one day to one year. The only exceptions were military commanders, who were elected to one-year terms, and holders of certain ancient priesthoods, who inherited their positions. The demos determined by vote whether or not anyone holding any public position was qualified to do his job, and after completion of his term, whether he had done it satisfactorily. All military commanders, and most holders of powerful allotted offices, came from the wealthy classes, but their success depended on the good will of the demos as a whole.

One of the most important allotted offices in the democracy was that of choregus, sponsor of a chorus. Choregi were allotted from a list of men wealthy enough to hold this office, for they had to recruit and pay for the training, costuming and room and board of the chorus that would perform at one of the festivals. In the case of a comic chorus this involved 24 dancers and the musicians who would accompany them. Being choregus gave a man an opportunity to display his wealth and refinement for the benefit of the demos as a whole and to win a prize that would confer prestige on himself and his dancers. Some wealthy men therefore volunteered to be a choregus instead of waiting for their names to be drawn. On the other hand, a man who put on a cheap or otherwise unsatisfactory chorus could expect to suffer a significant loss of public prestige.

All other festival expenses, including stipends for the poet and his actors and for prizes, were undertaken by vote of the demos and paid for from public funds. A poet got a place in the festival by submitting a draft some six months in advance to the office-holder in charge of the festival. Ancient sources say that at least the choral parts of the proposed play had to be submitted. How much more was submitted we do not know. But revision up to the day of the performance was certainly possible, since many allusions in comedy refer to events occurring very shortly before the festival: most notably the death of Sophocles shortly before the performance of *Frogs* in 405.

If he got on the program, the poet would be given his stipend and assigned his actors. He and the choregus would then set about getting the performance ready for the big day, the poet acting as music master, choreographer and director, the choregus rounding up, and paying the expenses of, the best dancers he could find. While tragic poets produced three tragedies and a satyr-drama, comic poets produced only one comedy.

Thus comedy, as a theatrical spectacle, was an organic feature of Athenian democracy. But its poetic, musical and mimetic traditions were much older, deriving from forms of entertainment developed by cultivated members of the aristocratic families that had governed Attica before the democracy. One such traditional form was the komos (band of revellers), which gave comedy (*komoidia* "song of the komos") its name. A komos was made up of some solidary group (a military, religious or family group, for example), often in masks or costumes, which entertained onlookers on many kinds of festive and religious occasions.

Part of the entertainment was abuse and criticism of individuals or groups standing outside the solidarity of the komos. The victims might be among the onlookers or they might be members of a rival komos. The komos sang and danced as a group, and its leader (who was no doubt also the poet) could speak by himself to his komos, to the onlookers or to a rival komos-leader. No doubt at a very early stage the komos was a competitive entertainment by which a given group could, in artistic ways, make those claims and criticisms against rival groups which at other times they might make in more overtly political ways. The targets of komastic abuse were often the village's most powerful men and groups. Thus the tradition of the komos was useful in allowing the expression of personal and political hostilities which would otherwise have been difficult to express safely: the misbehavior of powerful individuals, disruptive but unactionable gossip, the shortcomings of citizens in groups or as a whole. Here komos served a cathartic function, as a kind of social safety valve, allowing a relatively harmless airing of tensions before they could become dangerous, and also as a means of social communication and social control, upholding generally held norms and calling attention to derelictions.

But in addition to its critical and satiric aspects, komos (like all festive activities) had an idealistic side, encouraging people to envision the community as it would be if everyone agreed on norms and lived up to them, and a utopian side as well, allowing people to imagine how wonderful life would be if reality were as human beings, especially ordinary human beings, would like it to be. In this function komos provided a time-out from the cares and burdens of everyday life.

Old Comedies were theatrical versions of komos: the band of dancers with their leader was now a comic chorus involved in a story enacted by actors on a stage. The chorus still resembled a komos in two ways: (1) as performers, it competed against rival choruses, and (2) in its dramatic identity it represented, at least initially, a distinct group or groups: in *Birds*, for example, its members, each costumed as a different bird, represent and characterize the world of the birds. The comic chorus differs from a komos in that at any given point in a play it may drop its dramatic identity, since it always to some degree represents the festival's traditional comic chorus and thus reflects the celebrating community as a whole. In a comedy's choral parabasis (self-revelation) the chorus leader often steps forward, on behalf of the poet, to advise and admonish the spectators, and between episodes the chorus often sings abusive songs about particular individuals in the audience.

The actors in the stage-area had been amalgamated with the chorus during the sixth century. Their characteristic costumes (see Production, below) and antics were depicted in vase-paintings of that period in many parts of Greece, suggesting a much older tradition of comic mimesis. As early as the Homeric period (8th and 7th centuries) we find mythological burlesque and such proto-comedy as the Thersites-episode in the second book of the *Iliad*. In this period, too, the iambic poets flourished. Named for the characteristic rhythm of their verses, which also became the characteristic rhythm of actors in Athenian drama, the iambic poets specialized in self-revelation, popular story-telling, earthy gossip, and personal enmities, often creating fictitious first-person identities and perhaps also using masks and disguise. They were credited with pioneering poetic styles invective, obscenity and colloquialism.

The characters on the Old Comic stage preserved many of these traditions, but like the chorus they were an adaptation to the democratic festivals, most notably in political comedy. In Aristophanes's plays, the world depicted by the plot and the characters on stage was the world of the spectators in their civic roles: as heads of families and participants in governing the democratic state. We see the demos in its various capacities; the competitors for public influence; the men who hold or seek offices; the social, intellectual and artistic celebrities. We hear formal debate on current issues, including its characteristic invective. We get a decision, complete with winners and losers, and we see the outcome. This depiction of public life was designed both to arouse laughter and to encourage reflection about people and events in ways not possible in other public contexts. Thus it was at once a distorted and an accurate depiction of public life, somewhat like a modern political cartoon.

Aristophanic comedies typically depict Athens in the grip of a terrible and intractable problem (e.g. the war, bad political leaders, an unjust jury-system, dangerous artistic or intellectual trends), which is solved in a fantastic but essentially plausible way, often by a comic hero. The characters of these heroic plays fall into two main categories, sympathetic and unsympathetic. The sympathetic ones (the hero and his/her supporters) are fictitious creations embodying ideal civic types or representing ordinary Athenians. The unsympathetic ones embody disapproved civic behavior and usually represent specific leaders or categories of leaders. The sympathetic characters advocate positions held by political or social minorities and are therefore "outsiders." But they are shown winning out against the unsympathetic ones, who represent the current status quo. Characters or chorus-members representing the demos as a whole are portrayed as initially sceptical or hostile to the sympathetic character(s), but in the end they are persuaded; those responsible for the problem are disgraced or expelled; and Athens is recalled to a sense of her true (traditional) ideals and is thus renewed. In the (thoroughly democratic) comic view, the people are never at fault for their problems, but are merely good people who have been deceived by bad leaders. Thus the comic poets tried to persuade the actual demos (the spectators) to change its mind about issues that had been decided but might be changed (e.g. the war, as in *Acharnians* and *Lysistrata*), or to discard dangerous novelties (e.g. Socratic science and rhetoric, as in *Clouds*). Aristophanes at least once succeeded: after the performance of *Frogs* in 405 he was awarded a crown by the city for the advice that was given by the chorus-leader in that play and that was subsequently adopted by the demos.

In this way, the institution of Old Comedy performed functions essential to any democracy: public airing of minority views and criticism of those holding power. Thus the Old Comic festivals were in part a ritualized protest by ordinary people against its advisers and leaders. But they were also an opportunity to articulate civic ideals: one identified the shortcomings of the status quo by holding it up against a vision of things as they ought to (or used to) be. The use of satire and criticism within a plot addressing itself to important issues of national scope was thus a democratic adaptation of such pre-democratic traditions as komos and iambic poetry. That the comic festivals were state-run and not privately organized, a partnership between the elite and the masses, is striking evidence of the openness and self-confidence of a full democracy: the demos was completely in charge, so it did not fear attacks on its celebrities or resent admonition by the poets. In particular, the Athenians were much less inclined than we are to treat their political leaders with fear and reverence: since the Athenian people were themselves the government, they tended to see their leaders more as advisors and competitors for public stature than august representatives of the state. And even comic poets enjoyed the traditional role of Greek poets and orators generally: to admonish, criticise and advise on behalf of the people. In Socrates' case, the demos seems to have taken Aristophanes' criticisms to heart, however exaggerated they may have been: as Plato reported in his *Apology*, the *Clouds'* "nonsensical" portrait of Socrates was a factor in the people's decision, 24 years later, to condemn him to death.

The comic poets did not, however, enjoy a complete license to say anything they pleased: were that the case they could not have expected anyone to take what they had to say seriously. Following each festival there was an assembly in which anyone who had a legal complaint could come forward. Although the Athenians recognized freedom of speech, they did not tolerate any speech whatever. No one who spoke in public, comic poets included, could criticize the democratic constitution and the inherent rightness of the demos' rule, or say anything else that might in some way harm the democracy or compromise the integrity of the state religion. And abuse of individuals could not be slanderous. But the Athenian definition of slander differed from ours. Our slander laws are designed to protect individuals, whereas the Athenian slander laws were designed to protect the institutions of the democracy: they forbade malicious and unfounded abuse of individuals if and only if the abuse might compromise a man's civic standing or eligibility to participate in the democracy, for example, accusations that would, if taken seriously, make a man ineligible to participate in public life. And so, if the criticism and abuse we find in Old Comedy often seems outrageous by our standards, it is because we differ from the fifth-century Athenians in our definition of outrageous, not because comic poets were held to no standards.

Aristophanes, for example, was twice sued by the politician Cleon, once for slandering the demos and its officers in front of visiting foreigners (in *Babylonians* of 426) and once for slandering him (in *Knights* of 424). In the first instance the demos decided not to hear the case. In the second the poet and the politician settled out of court (in *Wasps* of 422 Aristophanes subsequently boasted that he had not abided by the agreement). The demos could also enact new laws restricting comic freedoms, to protect the integrity of the military or legal systems. One of these laws was enacted in 440, when Athens went to war against her own ally Samos; another, enacted in 415, forbade mention by name in comedy of any of the men who had recently been implicated in the parody of the Eleusinian Mysteries of Demeter. Possibly the demos wanted to protect from public innuendo those who might be suspected, but might not ultimately be convicted, of this crime: as we have seen, such innuendo would fall within the legal definition of slander. And possibly the demos did not want to take the chance that a comic poet might speak sympathetically of the profaners, as they often spoke for other underdogs; it is perhaps relevant that three of the men condemned seem to have been comic poets.

Production

Since fifth-century comic poets put on a play for a particular competition and did not envisage future productions, an original script that later circulated as a text for readers contained only the words, with few if any attributions of lines to speakers and no stage directions. These had to be inferred from the words of the text itself, so that all editions and translations, ancient and modern, differ to some extent in reconstructing the theatricality of the text. This means that anyone reading or performing an ancient comedy has a perfect right to bring the text to life in any way that seems appropriate: we have no information external to the text itself about how lines were originally distributed or performed, or about the original action on-stage and in the orchestra. Thus there can be no "authentic" productions of ancient comedies, only productions that strive, to a greater or lesser degree, to approximate what little we know of performance conditions at the time of their original production. In any case it is pointless to argue about "authenticity": in the end only satisfied spectators really count.

In this translation I assign speakers who seem to be the likeliest candidates for given lines; the reader is free to differ. I do not, however, supply stage-directions in the text itself: one of the pleasures of reading or performing an ancient comedy is imagining how it might be realized in action. I hesitate to put my own imagination in the way of a reader's, an actor's or a director's. But I do occasionally draw attention, in the notes, to likely action that is not quite obvious from the words of the text.

We do know some facts about fifth-century comic theater, however, and there is no harm in reviewing them for their historical interest.

Although Aristophanes' comedies are highly sophisticated as poetry and as drama, they nevertheless respected some ancient Dionysiac traditions that we should bear in mind if we want to respond to the characters in historical perspective. The actors wore masks, made of cork or papier-mâché, that covered the entire head. These were generic (young man, old woman, etc.) but might occasionally be special, like portrait-masks of prominent citizens (as in the case of Socrates in *Clouds*) or (as in *Birds*) of animals or gods. Although the characters' clothing was generically suited to their dramatic identities, mostly contemporary Greeks, there were several features that made them unmistakably comic: wherever possible, the costumes accommodated the traditional comic features of big stomach and rump and (for male characters) the grotesque costume penis called the phallos, made of leather, either dangling or erect as appropriate, and circumcised in the case of outlandish barbarians. Apparently by comic convention, male characters appearing without a phallos were marked as being in some way unmanly. And, as in every other dramatic genre, all roles were played by men. Even the naked females who often appear on stage, typically in the traditionally festive ending, were men wearing body-stockings to which false breasts and genitalia were attached. But the convention of all-male actors does not mean that Old Comedy was a kind of drag show: the same convention applied to all other kinds of drama as well (as it still did in Shakespeare's time), and nowhere in our comic texts is any female character ever understood to be anything but the character she is supposed to be, never a male playing a female.

The city supplied an equal number of actors to each competing poet, probably three, and these actors played all the speaking roles. In *Birds*, for example, there are 22 speaking roles, but the text's entrances and exits are so arranged that three actors can play them all. Some plays do, however, require a fourth (or even a fifth) actor in small roles. Perhaps in given years the allotment changed, or novices were periodically allowed to take small parts, or the poet or producer could add extra actors at his own expense.

In the orchestra ("dancing space") was a chorus of 24 men who sang and danced to the accompaniment of an aulos, a wind instrument that had two recorder-like pipes played simultaneously by a specially costumed player; and there could be other instruments as well. Like actors, members of the chorus wore masks and costumes appropriate to their dramatic identity. There could be dialogue between the chorus-leader and the actors on-stage, but the chorus as a whole only sings and dances. There was no ancient counterpart to the "choral speaking" often heard in modern performances of Greek drama. The choral songs of comedy were in music and language usually in a popular style, though serious styles were often parodied, and the dancing was expressive, adding a visual dimension to the words and music.

The stage-area was a slightly raised platform behind the large orchestra. Behind it was a wooden two-story building called the *skene* ("tent", from which our word "scene"). It had two or three doors at stage-level, windows at the second story, and a roof on which actors could appear. On the roof was a crane called the *mechane* ("machine"), on which actors could fly above the stage (as gods, for example, whence the Latin expression *deus ex machina*, "god from the machine"). Another piece of permanent equipment was a wheeled platform called the *ekkyklema* ("device for rolling out"), on which actors and scenery could be wheeled on-stage from the skene to reveal "interior" action. A painted or otherwise decorated plywood facade could be attached to the skene if a play (or scene) required it, and movable props and other scenery were used as needed. Since plays were performed in daylight in a large outdoor amphitheater, all entrances and exits of performers and objects took place in full view of the spectators. All in all, more demand was made on the spectators' imagination than in modern illusionistic theater, so that performers must often tell the spectators what they are supposed to see.

A fifth-century comedy was played through without intermission, the performance probably lasting about two hours. The usual structure of a comedy was a Prologue (actors); the Parodos, or entry, of the chorus into the orchestra (chorus); an Agon, or contest (actors and chorus); the Parabasis, or self-revelation, of the chorus (chorus-leader and chorus); and a series of episodes (actors) articulated by choral songs (chorus). In some plays, like *Birds*, there can be a second parabasis and/or a second agon. In this translation I have supplied appropriate divisions of the action, but performers should, as always, feel free to arrange their own performance as they see fit.

The Translation

I have translated the play into contemporary American verse, speakability being the principal stylistic criterion; the translation is designed for both readers and performers, and presupposes no knowledge of classical Greece or classical Greek theater. I render the Greek text line by line so as to give a sense of its original scope and pace. Where the original text refers to people, places, things and events whose significance modern audiences cannot reasonably be expected to know or to infer from the text, or which are inessential to its main point, I have tried to find easily comprehensible alternatives that preserve the import of the original. What may be unfamiliar in the text is explained in footnotes.

The conventions of Aristophanic comedy included the frank portrayal and discussion of religion, politics and sex (including nudity and obscenity). I have reproduced this feature as accurately as possible within my general guideline of easy intelligibility. To do otherwise would be to falsify the plays. After all, these three areas are of as fundamental importance to Greek society as they are to any society; and one of Aristophanes' chief aims was to make humor of them while at the same time encouraging his audience to think about them in ways discouraged, or even forbidden, outside the comic theater. The issue of freedom of speech and thought (especially religious and moral thought) is especially relevant to Aristophanes' plays; it is important to bear in mind that one of the hallmarks of Aristophanic comedy is to make us uncomfortable with the status quo. For those made uncomfortable by such provocative theater, these plays provide an opportunity to ask themselves why.

Since this translation is designed to be perfectly comprehensible to contemporary readers, the best way to stage it is to make it just as comprehensible to the audience for whom it was to be performed, using whatever human and other resources are available. Balloons, for example, make perfectly good comic phalloi, and music for the songs and moves for the dancers can be as simple or elaborate as one cares to make them. Adaptations of characters, and insertion of allusions to current events, make for liveliness (Aristophanes himself did this), and if the intended audience knows little about classical Athens, a modern producer may insert explanatory material or devise some other topical adaptation without violating any sort of standard of authenticity. The best guides for performance are the texts themselves.

This translation is based on the Greek text in my Loeb Classical Library edition (forthcoming); for textual and interpretive matters of all kinds I am much indebted to the editions with commentary by Alan H. Sommerstein (Warminster 1987) and Nan V. Dunbar (Oxford 1995).

Birds and its Time

Birds, produced at the Dionysia of 414 and winner of the second prize, is considered by many to be Aristophanes' masterpiece. It is the longest surviving comedy from antiquity, with the most adult speaking roles (22); it has a spectacular chorus, each of whose 24 dancers apparently represented a different bird;[1] the lyrics are among the most elaborate and lovely that Aristophanes ever wrote; and the fantasy is truly ethereal.

Information about Aristophanes' career becomes scanty for the years between *Peace* (Dionysia 421) and *Birds*, the period of the Peace of Nicias, which had brought to an uneasy close the first ten years of the great

---

1 Although the vase on the cover of this translation (Malibu, the J. Paul Getty Museum 82.AE.83), if it represents our play, shows identically costumed birds.

Peloponnesian War between Athens and Sparta. In this period there is no sign of the partisan political engagement, sometimes very fierce, that had animated the plays he wrote during the 420's, and the datable fragments point to mythological and other relatively apolitical subjects. Certainly the political environment had changed. Though the Peace of Nicias was not a true peace (the signatories remained mutually suspicious, and not all of Sparta's allies subscribed), Athens and its empire were quiet enough that "demagogic" politics, Aristophanes' favorite theme in the 420s, had fallen into abeyance. The political arena was instead dominated by the dashing young aristocrat, Alcibiades, now making his first bid for ascendancy, and the wealthy Nicias, a veteran general and conservative stalwart. Their backgrounds, rival policies, and contrasting styles offered great comic potential, but both were rightists hostile to "demagogues" (in 416 they colluded in the ostracism of the popular leader Hyperbolus), and so neither was much bothered by the comic poets, who in general show rightist biases.

Birds fits this trend. Its plot does follow a pattern familiar from Aristophanes' other "heroic" plays—a complaint, a fantastic idea, its implementation following a contest, episodes exemplifying the consequences, and the hero's utopian triumph[2]—but it differs from all of Aristophanes' other extant fifth-century plays in taking no topical issue, political or otherwise, as a theme, either expressly or, like *Knights* and *Wasps*, allegorically. To be sure, there is plenty of topical satire, but all of it is incidental to a fantasy that soars above the world's particulars to a conjured realm, where the most familiar hierarchies of empirical reality—earth and sky, nature and culture, polis and wilds, humans, animals, and gods—are blurred, reordered, or even abolished, and whose hero attains power surpassing even that of the gods.

Two old Athenians, Euelpides ("Confident") and Peisetaerus ("Persuader of His Comrade(s)"), have abandoned Athens in order to escape their debts. Led by a jackdaw and a crow, they visit Tereus, once a man but now a bird,[3] to learn if on his flights he has ever seen a carefree polis where they could settle. But none of Tereus' suggestions proves satisfactory, for no polis is carefree. Peisetaerus then asks about the life of the birds, which is carefree but lacks a polis. Suddenly he has an astonishing idea: to turn the scattered bird world into a mighty bird polis. Tereus summons the birds, represented by the Chorus. Being inveterate enemies of humankind, the birds are initially hostile, but Peisetaerus wins them over by pointing out that they were the original kings of the universe, long before the Olympians took over, and by proposing a plan: the birds will build an aerial city that com-

---

2 There is, however, greater structural unity than in earlier plays: Aristophanes maintains suspense by postponing the denouement until the end, and the momentum of the plot by having the Chorus Leader deliver the parabasis wholly in character.

3 Only this element of Tereus' myth is relevant; its violent details (15 n.) are ignored.

pletely occupies the sky; demand that the Olympians return power to them or face a blockade; and instruct humankind to sacrifice henceforth to the birds, for birds have the power to harm humans if they refuse, but also to give them every blessing if they accept. The birds are delighted with this plan and appoint Peisetaerus their leader; a magical root will give him wings. In the parabasis the Chorus Leader offers a cosmogony justifying the birds' claim to cosmic primogeniture.

Peisetaerus reappears newly winged, and names his new polis Cloudcuckooland. But scarcely has he begun the founding sacrifice when a parade of pests and profiteers, most of them satirizing familiar Athenian types, arrive seeking admission to the new polis; but none are admitted. Meanwhile, Iris (Rainbow), messenger of the gods, is intercepted on her way to humankind to announce Zeus' command for a resumption of sacrifices; Peisetaerus contemptuously turns her back. Finally an embassy from the Olympian gods arrives to negotiate a settlement. But Peisetaerus, secretly aided by Prometheus,[4] talks them into complete surrender: Zeus will return his scepter to the birds, and to Peisetaerus hand over his thunder bolt and his regal power, personified by a maiden, Princess Basileia ("Sovereignty"). In the finale, the Chorus praise and congratulate Peisetaerus as he weds Basileia and becomes the new king of the universe.

The fantasy of *Birds*, though set far from Athens, nevertheless fits the utopian mold of *Acharnians* and *Peace*, where the hero expels, excludes or renders harmless those forces human, natural, or divine that frustrate personal happiness and/or impede the common welfare; in this respect Cloudcuckooland is a cosmic avatar of Dicaeopolis' marketplace in *Acharnians*, a utopian counter-Athens. Peisetaerus too remains very much a contemporary Athenian in his restlessness, his enterprising cleverness, his visionary ideas, his persuasive skill, and his expansive dreams of power. Like previous comic heroes he wins the freedom to have things his own way and to enjoy untrammeled feasting and sex, but it is also made clear that everyone else—birds, humans, and even the gods—are better off under his new regime than they had been under the old.[5]

Some critics view Peisetaerus' new regime as a sinister affair, along the lines of Orwell's *Animal Farm*. But this requires that we view the play as wholly ironic (a technique unparalleled in ancient comedy), for on any straightforward reading we are always encouraged to identify with Peisetaerus, and therefore to approve of what he does. There is no sign of a coming fall (as in *Clouds*), no qualms or disapproval from the Chorus or any sympathetic character. Nor is there anything that would strike the average spectator as self-evidently sinister. Burlesque treatments of the gods,

---

4 A traditional defender of humankind against Zeus, and a god held in great affection at Athens.

5 Cf. especially 610, 1271-1307, 1605-15, 1726-30.

for example, and expressions of dissatisfaction with their rule are hardly rare in Attic drama, and Peisetaerus' remark that he is roasting "some birds who have been convicted of attempted rebellion against the bird democracy" (1583-85) is merely an incidental joke about the previous year's tyranny-scare and spate of prosecutions in Athens,[6] and is of no importance to the plot of the play.

Nevertheless, the grandiosity of Peisetaerus' ambition, his subversion of the natural order of things, and his crowning apotheosis may fairly be thought hubristic even for a comic hero. But in the spring of 414 the same can be said of the popular mood in Athens. The previous summer a great Athenian expedition had been dispatched, on the advice of Alcibiades, to conquer Sicily. According to Thucydides, who remarks on the expedition's "astonishing audacity" (6.31), the majority of Athenians were stricken with "lust" for the power and wealth that this conquest would bring, were absolutely confident (*euelpides*) of success, and were so excessively enthusiastic as to view opponents of the expedition as disloyal to the city (6.24). Nor were their spirits dampened even after a year of limited success in Sicily, the recall of Alcibiades from the command on a charge of impiety, and his subsequent defection to Sparta; on the contrary, they dispatched a second expedition to reinforce the first, and a few months after the performance of *Birds* even sent troops into Laconia in support of Argos (6.105), finally ending the Peace of Nicias.

The allusions to current events in *Birds* reflect this popular optimism: Nicias is praised for his strategic skill at Syracuse (363) and chided for delays (639); a would-be father-beater is sent to the Thracian front (1360-71); the reduction of Melos in 416, one of the most ominous episodes in Thucydides (5.84-111) and forever remembered as an example of imperial excess, is the subject of a casual joke (186), as is the outlawry of Alcibiades (145-47). The Athenians were now at the peak of their power and confidence, with no inkling that within two years their great armada was to be utterly destroyed and their very survival cast into doubt.

General Bibliography

Ancient sources for the production of classical drama are collected and discussed in:

Csapo, E. and Slater, W.J. *The Context of Ancient Drama* (Ann Arbor 1995)

Green, J.R. *Theatre in Ancient Greek Society* (London and New York 1994)

Pickard-Cambridge, A.W. *Dithyramb, Tragedy and Comedy*, rev. by T.B.L. Webster (Oxford 1962)

---

6 For which see Thucydides 6.53-61.

_____ *The Dramatic Festivals of Athens*, rev. by J. Gould and D.M. Lewis (Oxford 1968, rev. 1988)

Taplin, O. *Comic Angels and Other Approaches to Greek Drama through Vase-Paintings* (Oxford 1993)

Walcot, P. *Greek Drama in its Theatrical and Social Context* (Cardiff 1976)

Webster, T.B.L. *Greek Theatre Production* (London 1970)

Good general treatments of Aristophanic comedy are:

Arnott, P. *Greek Scenic Conventions in the Fifth Century B.C.* (Oxford 1962)

Bowie, A.M. *Aristophanes. Myth, Ritual and Comedy* (Cambridge 1993)

Cartledge, P. *Aristophanes and his Theatre of the Absurd* (London 1990)

Dobrov, G.W., ed. *The City as Comedy. Society and Representation in Athenian Drama* (Chapel Hill and London 1997)

Dover, K.J. *Aristophanic Comedy* (California 1972)

Harriott, R.M. *Aristophanes, Poet and Dramatist* (Baltimore 1986)

Hubbard, T.K. *The Mask of Comedy. Aristophanes and the Intertextual Parabasis* (Ithaca 1991)

MacDowell, D.M. *Aristophanes and Athens* (Oxford 1995)

McLeish, K. *The Theatre of Aristophanes* (New York 1980)

Moulton, C. *Aristophanic Poetry* (Hypomnemata 68: Göttingen 1981)

Reckford, K.J. *Aristophanes' Old-and-New Poetry* (Chapel Hill 1987)

Russo, C.F. *Aristophanes, an Author for the Stage* (London 1994)

Sifakis, G. *Parabasis and Animal Choruses* (London 1971)

Sommerstein, A.H. et al., eds. *Tragedy, Comedy and the Polis* (Bari 1993)

Stone, L.M. *Costume in Aristophanic Comedy* (New York 1981)

Whitman, C.H. *Aristophanes and the Comic Hero* (Cambridge MA 1964)

Winkler, J.J. and Zeitlin, F.I., eds. *Nothing to Do With Dionysos? Athenian Drama in its Social Context* (Princeton 1990)

Suggestions for Further Reading on *Birds*

Readers interested in the Greek text of *Birds* are referred to the editions by Sommerstein and Dunbar mentioned above.

The best ancient background reading for *Birds* is Thucydides' *History of the Peloponnesian War*, especially books 6-7.

Good interpretive treatments of the play in English in recent times, with further bibliography, include:

Arrowsmith, W. "Aristophanes' *Birds*: The Fantasy Politics of Eros," *Arion* 1 (1973) 119-67

Dobrov, G.W. "Language, Fiction, and Utopia," in Dobrov (above) 95-132

Gelzer, Th. "Some Aspects of Aristophanes' Comic Art in *Birds*," *Bulletin of the Institute of Classical Studies* 23 (1976) 1-14

Henderson, J. "Mass versus Elite and the Comic Heroism of Peisetaerus," in Dobrov (above) 135-48

Hubbard, T.K. "Utopianism and the Sophistic City in Aristophanes," in Dobrov (above) 23-50

Konstan, D. "The Greek Polis and its Negations: Versions of Utopia in Aristophanes' *Birds*," in Dobrov (above) 3-22

Romer, F.E. "Good Intentions and the *hodos he es korakas*," in Dobrov (above) 51-74

Slater, N.W. "Performing the City in *Birds*," in Dobrov (above) 75-94

Aristophanes' Birds

CHARACTERS

SPEAKING CHARACTERS

Euelpides, an Athenian
Peisetaerus, an Athenian
Slave of Tereus
Tereus, turned hoopoe
Priest
Poet
Oracle Collector
Meton
Inspector, from Athens
Decree Seller
First Messenger

Second Messenger
Iris
First Herald
Father Beater
Cinesias, a dithyrambic poet
Informer
Prometheus
Poseidon
Heracles
Triballian, a god
Second Herald

SILENT CHARACTERS

Xanthias and
Manodorus/Manes, Slaves
  of Euelpides and Peisetaerus
Slaves of Tereus
Flamingo, a bird
Mede, a bird

Hoopoe, a bird
Gobbler, a bird
Procne, turned nightingale
Piper, costumed as a raven
Slaves, as archers and slingers
Princess

CHORUS of Birds

PROLOGUE

(Euelpides, Peisetaerus, Slave, Tereus)

Euelpides°
Is it straight ahead you're pointing us, toward that tree there?

Peisetaerus°
You blasted bird! This one keeps croaking "go back!"

---

1 A fictitious name meaning "Confident."
2 A fictitious name meaning "Persuader of His Comrade(s)."

Euelpides

You bastard, why all this trekking back and forth?
We're goners if we just wander an aimless path.

Peisetaerus

I'm pitiful! Imagine letting a crow convince me   5
to take a hike of more than a hundred miles!

Euelpides

And as for me, I'm hapless, letting a jackdaw
convince me to pound the nails right off my toes!

Peisetaerus

Now even I'm unsure where on earth we are.
Think you could find our native land from here?   10

Euelpides

God no, from here not even Execestides could!°

Peisetaerus

Damn!

Euelpides

        Travel your own side of the road, my friend.

Peisetaerus

He's really done us dirty, that man from the bird market
who sells by the tray, that crazy Philocrates.°
He claimed these two would point the way to Tereus,°   15
the hoopoe who once was human and became a bird;
and he sold us that Son of Tharreleides° there,
the jackdaw, for one obol, and this crow here for three.
But they turn out to know nothing at all but nipping.
What are you gaping at this time? Do you mean to take us   20
into these cliffs somewhere? There's no passage here.

Euelpides

My god, there isn't even a pathway here.

---

11 Athenian citizenship required native Athenian parents; Execestides (otherwise un-
    known) was evidently vulnerable to the charge of having Carian ancestry, cf. line 764.
14 To judge from lines 1076-1083, Philocrates (otherwise unknown) was a prominent
    wholesaler of birds.
15 In this myth, as dramatized by the tragic poet Sophocles probably in the late 430's,
    Tereus, King of Thrace, on his way to wed the Athenian princess Procne, raped her
    sister Philomela, whose tongue he cut out to prevent her from telling anyone. But she
    depicted the crime on an embroidery she sent to Procne, and the sisters avenged them-
    selves by serving Tereus' son Itys to him for dinner. When Tereus chased the sisters
    with a sword, the gods changed him into a hoopoe, Procne into a nightingale, and
    Philomela into a swallow. The nightingale's song was regarded as a lament for Itys.
17 Evidently a man resembling a jackdaw, which is small and noisy.

Peisetaerus
  This crow's saying something about the passage;
  oh yes indeed, it's croaking differently now.
Euelpides
  Well, what's it say about the passage, then?   25
Peisetaerus
  Oh nothing; just that it plans to bite off my fingers!
Euelpides
  Now isn't this a terrible situation!
  Just when we're both ready and eager to go
  straight to the buzzards, we can't even find the way!
  The thing is, you gentlemen there in the audience,   30
  we're sick with the opposite of Sacas'° sickness:
  see, he's a non-citizen trying to force his way in,
  while we, men of good standing in tribe and clan,
  solid citizens, with no one trying to shoo us away,
  have up and left our country with both feet flying.   35
  Now it's not that we hate the city of Athens *per se*,
  as if it weren't essentially great and blest,
  where all can watch their wealth fly away in fines.
  But the thing of the matter is, cicadas chirp
  on their boughs for only a month or two, while Athenians,   40
  they harp on their lawsuits all their livelong lives.
  That's why we're trekking this trek, and wandering
  with basket, kettle, and myrtle boughs° in search
  of a peaceable place, a place where we can settle
  down and simply pass our lives in peace.   45
  Our mission now is to see Tereus the Hoopoe;
  we need to learn from him if on his flights
  he's seen that sort of city anywhere.
Peisetaerus
  Hey!
Euelpides
      What is it?
Peisetaerus
          This crow's been trying for quite a while
  to show me something up there.

---

31 Sacas, "the Sacasian" (an Asian Scythian), was a nickname for the tragic dramatist
   Acestor, who had evidently had trouble certifying his Athenian citizenship.
43 Implements used ceremonially in founding a settlement.

Euelpides

                  This jackdaw here   50
has been gaping upwards too, as if pointing me
toward something. There must be birds in the area.
We'll soon find out, if we start to make some noise.

Peisetaerus

Say, why don't you thump that rock there with your leg?

Euelpides

You thump it with your head, we'll get twice the noise.   55

Peisetaerus

Then get a stone and knock.

Euelpides

                I will. Boy! Boy!

Peisetaerus

Hey, what are you saying? Calling the Hoopoe "boy"?
You should be calling "oh Hoopoe," not "hey boy."

Euelpides

Oh Hoopoe! You'll only make me keep knocking, you know.
Oh, Hoopoe!

Slave

             Who's there? Who's shouting for the master?   60

Peisetaerus

God save us, will you look at the size of that beak!

Slave

Oh heaven help me, here's a pair of birdnappers!

Peisetaerus

Imagine speaking so harshly, and not more politely!

Slave

You're dead!

Peisetaerus

             But we're not humans!

Slave

                      Then what are you?

Peisetaerus

Me? A yellowbelly; it's a Libyan bird.   65

Slave

What nonsense!

Peisetaerus

             Really? Then check the back of my legs.

Slave
And this other one, what kind of bird is he? Speak up.

Euelpides
Me? I'm a brownbottom, a bird from the Pheasance.

Peisetaerus
And what kind of creature are you, in heaven's name?

Slave
Me, I'm a slavebird.

Euelpides
                    Vanquished by some fighting   70
cock?

Slave
      No, it's just that when master became a hoopoe,
he prayed that I become a bird as well,
so that he could still have his butler and attendant.

Peisetaerus
Does a bird actually need to have some sort of butler?

Slave
He does, I guess because he once was human.   75
He'll get a craving for fish fry from Phalerum,
and I grab the pan and run out for the fish.
Or he'll want lentil soup, we need a ladle and tureen,
so I run for the tureen.

Peisetaerus
                  This one's a roadrunner.
So, roadrunner, know what you should do? Call out   80
your master.

Slave
             Oh goodness no; he's just started
his nap, after lunching on myrtle berries and gnats.

Peisetaerus
Wake him anyway.

Slave
             Well, I'm quite sure
he'll be annoyed, but as a favor I'll wake him.

Peisetaerus
And to hell with you, for scaring me to death!   85

Euelpides
Well I'll be damned, my jackdaw flew away
from me in terror!

Peisetaerus
>   You utter scaredy cat,
> so scared you let him go!

Euelpides
>   Say, didn't you
> fall down and let your own crow get away?

Peisetaerus
> I certainly didn't.

Euelpides
>   Then where is it?

Peisetaerus
>   It just flew off.   90

Euelpides
> So you didn't loose it, brave fellow that you are?

Tereus
> Unbar the woods, that I may at last come forth!

Peisetaerus
> Lord Heracles, what kind of beast is this?
> What kind of plumage? What manner of triple crest?

Tereus
> Who be those that seek me?

Euelpides
>   The Twelve Gods° seem   95
> to have made a mess of you.

Tereus
>   You wouldn't be mocking
> me for my plumage? For, friends, I'll have you know
> I once was human.

Peisetaerus
>   It's not you that's funny.

Tereus
>   What, then?

Euelpides
> It's that beak of yours that looks so funny to us.

Tereus
> That goes to show how shabbily Sophocles   100
> treats me—Tereus!—in his tragedies.°

---

95 The standard Olympian pantheon.
101 In Sophocles' play (see 15 n.) Tereus seems to have been portrayed as an uncouth
   barbarian.

Peisetaerus
So you're Tereus? Are you a bird or a peacock?

Tereus
Me, I'm a bird.

Euelpides
Then where do you keep your feathers?

Tereus
They've fallen out.

Euelpides
Because of some disease?

Tereus
No; all birds shed their feathers in wintertime,   105
and then we grow back new ones once again.
But tell me now who you two are.

Peisetaerus
We're humans.

Tereus
What nationality?

Peisetaerus
The land of lovely triremes.°

Tereus
Not jurors, I hope!°

Euelpides
Oh no, the other kind:
we're jurophobes.

Tereus
Does that seed sprout there?   110

Euelpides
You'll find some in the country, if you look hard.

Tereus
Now then, what business brings you two up here?

Peisetaerus
We want to confer with you.

Tereus
And what about?

---

108 That is, Athens.
109 Athenian litigiousness was a national joke; Aristophanes had explored it in his play
  Wasps of 422.

Peisetaerus
Well, originally you were human, just like us,
and once you owed people money, just like us,   115
and once you enjoyed not repaying it, just like us;
then trading all that for the guise of birds, you've flown
the circuit of land and sea, and your mind contains
everything a human's does, and everything
a bird's does too. That's why we've come to visit,   120
hoping you know of a nice cushy city, soft
as a woollen blanket, where we could curl up and relax.

Tereus
Could you be looking for a city greater than the Cranaans'?°

Peisetaerus
Not greater, no, just better suited to us.

Tereus
You're obviously looking for an aristocracy.   125

Peisetaerus
Who me? Not at all. Even Scellias' son makes me sick.°

Tereus
Then, what kind of city would you most prefer to live in?

Peisetaerus
One where my very worst troubles would be like this:
a friend appears at my door one morning and says,
"Now swear to me by Zeus the Olympian   130
that you and your kids will take a bath and be
at my place bright and early for a wedding feast.
Now please don't let me down, for otherwise
you needn't pay me a visit when I'm in trouble!"

Tereus
My word, it's miserable troubles that you long for!   135
And you?

Euelpides
                    I long for much the same.

Tereus
                                        Such as?

Euelpides
A city where the father of a blooming boy

---

123 Cranaus was a mythical king of Athens.
126 Aristocrates was a real politician and general, soon to be a supporter of oligarchy, but
here his name alone is the joke.

would meet me and complain like this, as if wronged:
"It's a dandy way you treat my son, Mr. Smoothy!
You met him leaving the gymnasium after his bath,   140
and you didn't kiss him, chat him up, or hug him,
or fondle his balls—and you my old family friend!"

Tereus

Poor thing, what troubles you long for! Well, there's actually
a happy city of the sort you two describe,
on the shores of the Red Sea.

Euelpides

                          Absolutely not!   145
No seaside for us, where the *Salaminia*°
will pop up one morning with a summonser on board.
Don't you know of a Greek city to tell us about?

Tereus

Why don't you go to Lepreus, in Elis,
and settle there?

Euelpides

                  God! Lepreus makes me sick,   150
though I've never seen it, because of Melanthius.°

Tereus

Well, then there's the Opuntii in Locris; you
should settle there.

Euelpides

                Not me; I wouldn't become
an Opuntius° if you gave me a talent of gold.

Peisetaerus

But what about this life with the birds? Describe it,   155
for you know every detail.

Tereus

                    It wears quite nicely.
To begin with, you must get by without a wallet.

Euelpides

A lot of life's fraudulence disappears right there.

---

146 One of two sacred galleys in the Athenian navy (the other was the *Paralus*) used for
    official dispatches and transport.

151 A tragic poet, who apparently suffered from the skin disease *lepra*.

154 A man by this name is mentioned as one-eyed at line 1294, and also as beak-nosed in
    other comedies.

Tereus
And in the gardens we feed on white sesame seeds,
and myrtle-berries, and poppies, and watermint.°   160

Euelpides
Why, you birds are living the life of honeymooners!

Peisetaerus
Aha, aha!
Oh what a grand scheme I see in the race of birds,
and power that could be yours, if you take my advice!

Tereus
What advice would that be?

Peisetaerus
                    What advice? For starters,
don't fly around aimlessly with your beaks agape;   165
that's discreditable behavior. For example,
back home, if among the flighty crowd you ask,
"Who's that guy over there?" Teleas° will reply,
"The man's an absolute bird—unstable, flighty,
unverifiable, never staying put."   170

Tereus
By Dionysus, that's a fair criticism.
Well, how can it be helped?

Peisetaerus
                    Found a single city.

Tereus
But what kind of city could mere birds ever found?

Peisetaerus
Oh really, what an utterly doltish remark!
Look down.

Tereus
                    Very well, I'm looking.

Peisetaerus
                              Now look up.   175

Tereus
I'm looking.

---

160 Items associated in Athenian life with festive occasions.
168 Probably the son of Telenicus, and currently serving as a Treasurer of Athena; a wealthy
   politician (cf. 1024-5) ridiculed elsewhere for gluttony, political trickery, and shifti-
   ness, among other faults. Here both the text and the point of the joke are uncertain.

Peisetaerus

        Turn your head around.

Tereus

                        By heaven,
I'll be making real progress, if I sprain my neck!

Peisetaerus

Did you see anything?

Tereus

                I saw the clouds and sky.

Peisetaerus

Well surely, then, you've seen the birds' own site.

Tereus

Their site? In what sense?

Peisetaerus

              As it were, their place.   180
It's a place to *visit*, where everything makes a *transit*,
so that's why now it's merely called a *site*.
But as soon as you settle in and fortify it,
this *site* will instead start being called a *city*.
And then you'll rule over humans as over locusts;   185
and as for the gods, you'll destroy them by Melian famine.°

Tereus

How?

Peisetaerus

    What's between them and the earth? Air, right?
Look, we have to ask the Boeotians for a visa
whenever we want to visit Delphi, no?
Alright, whenever humans sacrifice to the gods,   190
you won't let the aroma of the thigh-bones pass
through, unless the gods pay you some tribute.

Tereus

Oho, I get it!
I swear by earth, by snares, by gins, by nets,
I've never heard a more elegant idea!   195
And so I'm happy to help you found this city,
if that's agreeable to the other birds.

Peisetaerus

And who's going to explain the plan to them?

---

186 In summer 416 the Athenians had besieged the small island of Melos, and upon its
surrender exterminated the adult male population, for refusing to join the empire.

Tereus

You are.
I've long lived with them, and they're not the barbarians
they were before I taught them how to speak.   200

Peisetaerus
Then how will you call them together?

Tereus

Easily.
I'll just step right into my thicket here, and then
I'll rouse from sleep my own dear nightingale,°
and we'll invite them to come. And if they hear
our voice the birds will speed here on the double.   205

Peisetaerus
Then, dearest of birds, please don't just stand around;
I implore you, go step into the thicket there
as quick as you can and rouse the nightingale!

PARODOS°
(Tereus, Peisetaerus, Euelpides, Chorus)

Tereus
Come, my songmate, leave your sleep,
and loosen the strains of sacred songs,   210
that from your divine lips bewail
deeply mourned Itys, your child and mine,°
trilling forth fluid melodies
from your vibrant throat.
Pure the sound
that ascends through green-tressed bryony   215
to Zeus' abode, where gold-tressed
Phoebus° listens to your songs of grief
and, strumming in response his ivoried
lyre, stirs the gods to their dance;
and from deathless lips arises   220
in harmonious accord
the divine refrain of the Blest.

Euelpides
Lord Zeus almighty, what a voice that birdy
has! How it turned the entire thicket to honey!

203 Procne, cf. 46 n.
208 *Parodos* is the term applied to that section of an Aristophanic comedy in which the
   Chorus is introduced, enters the *orchestra*, and performs its first song and dance.
212 See 15 n.
217 Apollo.

Peisetaerus
  Hey there.

Euelpides
        Hey what?

Peisetaerus
              Be quiet!

Euelpides
                    Whatever for?   225

Peisetaerus
  The Hoopoe's getting ready to sing again.

Tereus
  Epopopoi popopopoi popoi,
  ye ye co co co co
  come ye hither every bird of fellow feather,

  all who range over country acres   230
  richly sown, the myriad tribes who feed on barleycorn,
  and the races of seed pickers
  that swiftly fly, casting a cozy cry;
  and all who oft round the clod
  in the furrow twitter delicately   235
  this happy sound,
  tio tio tio tio tio tio tio tio!

  And all of you who pasture on ivy boughs
  in the gardens,
  and you eaters of oleaster and arbutus   240
  in the hills,
  come flying at once to my call:
  trioto trioto totobrix!

  And you who in marshy vales snap up
  keen-mouthed gnats, and all who inhabit   245
  the earth's drizzly places and Marathon's lovely meadow,°
  and the bird with dappled plumage,
  francolin, francolin!
  And all whose tribes fly with the halcyons
  over the deep swell of the sea,   250
  come hither to learn the latest!
  Yes, here we're gathering all the tribes

---

246 Lovely only to birds, since Marathon (a deme 26 miles from Athens) was swampy and buggy.

of neck-stretching birds,
for an acute old man has appeared,
novel in ideas   255
and a doer of novel deeds.

Now all attend the conference,
hither hither hither hither!
Torotorotorotorotix,   260
kikkabau kikkabau,
torotorotorolililix!

Peisetaerus
Do you see any birds?

Euelpides
                    I certainly don't,
though I'm all agape from looking at the sky.

Peisetaerus
Then it seems the Hoopoe copied the curlew bird,   265
entering the thicket and crying hoo-poo for nothing.

Tereus
Torotix torotix!

Euelpides
Maybe so, my friend, but look over here, a bird is coming!°

Peisetaerus
That's a bird all right! Whatever can it be? Surely not a peacock?

Euelpides
Our host here will tell us himself. Say, what kind of bird is that?   270

Tereus
Not one of those commonplace birds you humans are used to seeing;
he's a bird of the marshes.

Euelpides
                    My, how flamboyantly crimson he is!

Tereus
That stands to reason, because in fact his name is Flamingo.

Euelpides
Ho there, psst—yes, you!

Peisetaerus
                    What do you want?

---

268 The switch to long verses indicates the beginning of the *parodos* proper (209 n.).

Euelpides

Here's another bird!

Peisetaerus

Oh yes, there's another one, and he's also garbed in eccentric color. 275
Now who can this vatic songster be, this outlandish mountain-
walker?

Tereus

This bird's called a Mede.

Euelpides

A Mede? Lord Heracles!
But if he's really a Mede, how did he fly here without a camel? °

Peisetaerus

Here's still another bird who's secured itself a crest.

Euelpides

What's this apparition? You mean you're not the only hoopoe,   280
this other's a hoopoe too?

Tereus

He's the son of Philocles' hoopoe,°
and I'm his grandfather, the same as you might say
Hipponicus son of Callias and Callias son of Hipponicus.°

Peisetaerus

So this bird is Callias. He's shed a lot of feathers.

Tereus

He's pedigreed, you see, so he gets plucked by shysters,   285
and the females too keep plucking away his plumage.

Euelpides

Lord Poseidon! Here's still another brightly tinted bird.
What on earth is this one called, I wonder?

Tereus

That one? Gobbler.

Peisetaerus

You mean there's another gobbler besides Cleonymus?°

---

278 The Athenians had not forgotten that the Medes (a people who inhabited what is
now NW Iran) had used camels in their invasion of Greece in 480.

281 Philocles, nephew of Aeschylus and nicknamed "The Lark" (?476, 1295), wrote a
tragic tetralogy *Pandionis*, which included Tereus' metamorphosis.

283 For five generations the heads of one wealthy and distinguished family of the Ceryces
clan had alternated these names; the current Callias was often ridiculed as a flagrant
wastrel.

289 A politician often ridiculed for obesity, gluttony, and effeminacy, and (uniquely) for
having thrown away his shield in battle (see lines 1470-81).

Euelpides
>If that were really Cleonymus, he'd surely have tossed his crest?   290

Peisetaerus
>But I can't imagine what's the point of the birds' cresting?
>Preparing for the race in arms?°

Tereus
>   Oh no, my friend,
>they're like the Carians: they nest on crests for safety's sake.°

Peisetaerus
>Poseidon, will you look at that! What a hell of a mob
>of birds has gathered!°

Euelpides
>   Lord Apollo, what a cloud of them! Whooee!   295
>They're so many a-wing that you can't see into the wings anymore!

Peisetaerus
>That one's a partridge.

Euelpides
>   And by god that one's a francolin.

Peisetaerus
>And that one's a wigeon.

Euelpides
>   And that one's a halcyon.

Peisetaerus
>So what's that one behind her?

Euelpides
>   That one there? A snippet.

Peisetaerus
>You mean there's a snip-it bird?

Euelpides
>   Isn't Sporgilus one?°   300
>And there's an owl.

Peisetaerus
>   Say what? Who's brought an owl to Athens?°

---

292 A footrace of about 370 meters in which the runners wore helmets (crested) and carried shields.
293 Many towns in Caria (an area in SW Asia Minor) had hilltop citadels.
294 Enter the Chorus, each member costumed as a different bird.
300 Sporgilus ("Sparrow") was the name of a barber.
301 Proverbial, like "coals to Newcastle."

Euelpides
Jay. Turtledove. Lark. Reed Warbler. Thyme-finch. Rock Dove.
Vulture. Hawk. Ring Dove. Cuckoo. Redshank. Red-head Shrike.
Porphyrion. Kestrel. Dabchick. Bunting. Lammergeier. Woodpecker.

Peisetacrus
Whooee, all the birds! Whooee, all the peckers!   305
Oh how they peep and run around, outscreeching each another!
Say, can they be threatening us? Oh dear, they've certainly got
their beaks open, and they're staring at you and me!

Euelpides
                         I think so too!

Chorus
Whe-whe-whe-whe-whe-whe-where's the one who called me?
   What spot is he settled on?   310

Tereus
Here I am ready and waiting, and not aloof from friends.

Chorus
Wha-wha-wha-wha-wha-wha-what message then
   have you got for your friends?   315

Tereus
One concerning us all, promoting our security, right, gratifying,
   advantageous!
You see, two men are here to visit me, a pair of subtle thinkers.

Chorus
Where? How? What do you mean?

Tereus
I say, a pair of old men are here from the human world,   320
and they've come bearing the prop of a prodigious plan.

Chorus Leader
Oh, you've made the worst blunder since I was fledged!
What did you say?

Tereus
             Don't be flustered yet.

Chorus Leader
                     What have you done to us?

Tereus
I've received two men passionately enamored of our society.

Chorus Leader
You've actually done this?

Tereus

Yes I have, and I'm glad I did.   325

Chorus Leader

And they're already somewhere among us?

Tereus

As sure as I'm among you.

FIRST CONTEST (AGON)°
(Chorus, Chorus Leader, Peisetaerus, Euelpides, Tereus)

Chorus (strophe)°

Oo, oo!

We are betrayed, we are impiously defiled!

Yes, our former friend, who browsed with us

in the fields that feed us all,   330

has broken our ancient ordinances,

has broken our avian oaths.

He's lured me into a trap,

he's cast me out among an unholy race,

that since its very creation

has been groomed to be my foe.   335

Chorus Leader

Well, him we'll settle accounts with at a later time;

as for these two codgers, I think they should give us satisfaction

on the spot, by being dismembered.

Peisetaerus

So we're goners.

Euelpides

This damned mess we're in is all your fault, you know!

Why did you bring me here from back there?

Peisetaerus

To keep me company.   340

---

327 The *Agon*, or formal debate, is a standard structural feature of Old Comedy consisting of formal arguments in long-verses by two contestants, each argument prefaced by a choral song and an introduction by the chorus leader; the chorus leader usually presides and may (along with the idle contestant) interject comments or questions to break up or otherwise enliven the long speeches.

327 The songs and dances performed in the orchestra by a Greek dramatic chorus were normally strophic, that is, they were composed in two or more strophes (stanzas) that "respond" (have the same rhythmical structure); the first song in a responding pair is called the strophe, the second the antistrophe.

Euelpides
    To make me cry bitter tears, you mean!

Peisetaerus
                                You're talking rot;
    how do you expect to cry once you've had your eyes pecked out?

Chorus (antistrophe)
    Hi ho!
    Forward march, launch a hostile
    bloody charge, from all sides   345
    put wings to them and surround them!
    For both these two must howl
    and furnish fodder for my beak.
    For there's no dusky mountain,
    no lofty cloud, no leaden sea
    to receive this pair   350
    in flight from me.

Chorus Leader
    Now without further ado let's pluck and peck these two.
    Where's the lieutenant? Have him bring up the right wing.

Euelpides
    This is it! Poor goner, where can I hide?

Peisetaerus
                                Hold your ground there!

Euelpides
    And let them dismember me?

Peisetaerus
                                But how do you expect   355
    to get away?

Euelpides
        I've no idea.

Peisetaerus
                Well, here's what we should do:
    we should stand and fight, and make use of some of those kettles!

Euelpides
    What good will a kettle do us?

Peisetaerus
                                It'll keep the owls away.

Euelpides
    But what about those with the hooked talons there?

Peisetaerus

Grab a skewer
and plant it in front of you.

Euelpides

And what about our eyes? 360

Peisetaerus

Take out a saucer and shield them with it, or a bowl.

Euelpides

Oh brilliant! A fine piece of improvisation and generalship.
In clever strategems you've already outstripped Nicias!°

Chorus Leader

Ta dum ta da! Move out, level your beaks, no hanging back!
Drag, pluck, hit and flay them! First knock out the kettle! 365

Tereus

Say, you scurviest of all creatures, why do you aim
to destroy and mutilate two men who've done you no harm,
who are my wife's kinsmen and fellow tribesmen?°

Chorus Leader

You're saying these men merit any more mercy than wolves?
What enemies could we take revenge on more hateful than these? 370

Tereus

But suppose they're enemies by nature, yet friends by intention,
and they've come here to give you some beneficial instruction?

Chorus Leader

How could these men ever give us any beneficial instruction
or advice? They were already enemies of our very forefeathers!

Tereus

And yet the wise can learn a lot from their enemies. 375
Caution does save the day—a lesson you can't learn
from a friend, but the very first lesson an enemy imposes.
For instance, it was from enemies, not friends, that cities
learned to erect lofty walls and master warships,
and it's that lesson that safeguards children, household,
and property. 380

Chorus Leader

Well, in our opinion it's possible to hear them out first;
the wise can discover some benefit even from enemies.

---

363 Probably a reference to that general's victory at Syracuse the previous autumn.
368 Procne (see 15 n.) was the daughter of the legendary Athenian king, Pandion.

Peisetaerus
They look to be slackening their anger. Fall back by steps.

Tereus
Besides, it's only fair, and plus, you owe me one.

Chorus Leader
Well, we've surely never opposed you in anything before.   385

Euelpides
They're acting more peaceable.

Peisetaerus
Indeed they are. So lower the kettle
and the two bowls;
and we should shoulder the spear—
I mean the skewer—and walk patrol   390
inside our encampment, looking along
the very rim of the kettle,
close in, since we mustn't run away.

Euelpides
But tell me, if we do get killed,
where on earth will we be buried?

Peisetaerus
Potter's Field will take us.°   395
You see, we'll get a state funeral
by telling the generals
that we died fighting the enemy
at the Battle of Finchburg.°

DUET
(Chorus Leader, Tereus)

Chorus Leader
Re-form ranks as before,   400
lean over and ground your temper
alongside your anger, like infantrymen;
and let's find out who these men may be,
where they've come from,
and with what in mind.   405
Hey there, Hoopoe, I'm calling on you!

---

395 The Cerameicus, the potters' quarter of Athens where military funerals were held.
399 In the previous year an Athenian contingent had assisted in the siege of Orneae
(*orneon* "bird"), a town in the Argolid, but its defenders slipped away and there was
no battle.

Tereus
And what is your wish in calling?

Chorus Leader
Who may these men be, and whence?

Tereus
Two strangers from clever Greece.

Chorus Leader
And what chance   410
can have brought them
on a journey to the birds?

Tereus
A passionate desire
for your way of life,
to share your home
and be with you completely!

Chorus Leader
What do you mean?
And what tales is he telling?   415

Tereus
Incredible and beyond belief.

Chorus Leader
Does he see a way to cash in on his visit,
convinced that being with me
he'll overpower his enemy
or be able to help his friends?   420

Tereus
He promises great prosperity, ineffable
and incredible, for
he makes a convincing case
that you can have it all—what's here,
and there, and everywhere.   425

Chorus Leader
Is he insane?

Tereus
Oh, how unutterably sane!

Chorus Leader
There's wisdom in his heart?

Tereus
He's the craftiest fox,
all cleverness, a go-getter, a smoothie, the crème de la craft!   430

Chorus Leader
Tell him to speak, to speak!
For as I listen to the tale you tell
I'm all aflutter.

EPISODE
(Tereus, Peisetaerus, Euelpides, Chorus Leader)

Tereus
All right then, you and you take my panoply
back inside and hang it in the kitchen—   435
knock on wood—by the trivet. And you inform
and brief these birds about the proposals I summoned
them to hear.
Peisetaerus
    By god, I'll do nothing of the kind,
not unless they promise me the very same deal
as once upon a time the monkey made   440
with his woman, you know, the knifemaker:° that they're not
to bite me or yank my balls or poke my—
Euelpides
                  You
can't mean the—
Peisetaerus
        Not at all; the eyes, I meant to say.
Chorus Leader
Then that's a promise.
Peisetaerus
        Now swear to me you'll keep it!
Chorus Leader
So help me a victory by unanimous vote   445
of all the judges and the audience—°
Peisetaerus
        Amen!
Chorus Leader
but if I lie, to win by only one vote.

---

440 The various guesses in the scholia show that not even ancient scholars could explain
    this allusion.
445 Momentarily speaking as a performer in the dramatic competition.

Peisetaerus
   Now hear this: the infantry may retrieve
   their arms and go back home, but should keep an eye
   on the boards for any notices we may post.   450

SECOND CONTEST (AGON)
(Chorus, Chorus Leader, Peisetaerus, Euelpides)

Chorus (strophe)
   A treacherous thing every time in every way
   is human nature. But do make your case, for perhaps
   you may divulge a good quality that you see in me
   or some greater potential   455
   overlooked by my witless mind.
   Explain to us all this perception of yours,
   for whatever advantage you may provide me
   will be an advantage for us all.

Chorus Leader
   Now then, about this idea of yours that you've come to sell us: 460
   explain it, and never fear, we won't break the truce till you do.

Peisetaerus
   Well, I'm bursting to tell you, and I've got a special speech
         whipped up,
   which nothing stops me from kneading into cake. A garland, boy,
   and water for my hands, right now.

Euelpides
                           We having dinner, or what?

Peisetaerus
   No no, I've long been trying to make a big juicy utterance   465
   that will shatter these birds to the very soul. So sorrowful am I
   for you, who once were kings—

Chorus Leader
                           Us kings? Of what?

Peisetaerus
                           Yes you,
   of all that exists, from yours truly up to Zeus himself,
   and born a long time before Cronus, and the Titans, and even Earth.°

Chorus Leader
   Even Earth?

---

467 Peisetaerus appeals to the standard divine succession-myth, for which see Hesiod,
   Theogony 133-210.

Peisetaerus
> Yes, by Apollo.

Chorus Leader
> I certainly never heard that.   470

Peisetaerus
> You're just ignorant and uninquisitive, and you haven't thumbed
>   your Aesop.°
> He says in his fable that the Lark was the first of all birds to be born,
> before Earth; and then her father perished of a disease,
> but there being no earth, he'd lain out for four days° and she
>   didn't know
> what to do, till in desperation she buried her father in her
>   own head.   475

Euelpides
> So that's why to this day the Lark's father lies dead in the Head.°

Peisetaerus
> So if they were born before Earth and before the gods, it would follow
> that the kingship is rightfully theirs by primogeniture!

Chorus Leader
> By Apollo, it does.

Euelpides
> Then you should plan on growing a beak,
> for Zeus won't be quick to return his sceptre to the woodpecker!   480

Peisetaerus
> Now then, it didn't used to be gods who ruled mankind
> and were kings, but birds, and I have lots of evidence for this.
> I'll start by showing you that the cock first ruled and reigned
> over the Persians, before all those Dariuses and Megabazuses,°
> and that's why he's still called the Persian Bird, in memory of
>   that reign.   485

Euelpides
> So that's why to this day he struts about like the Great King,
> the only bird who gets to wear his hat cocked!

---

471 The legendary animal fabulist, thought to have lived in early sixth-century Samos.
474 In Athens the "laying out" was held the day after death, and burial the following
     morning.
476 The deme Cephale ("Head") was the site of a large cemetery. There is perhaps an-
     other reference to Philocles the Lark (281 n.).
484 Darius I reigned 522-486 and was repulsed by the Athenians at Marathon in 490;
     Megabazus (in Greek the name suggests "big-talker") was a commander during his
     reign.

Peisetaerus
So powerful, so great and mighty was he, that to this very day,
as a result of that long-ago power, he has only to sing reveille
and everyone jumps up to work: smiths, potters, tanners, cobblers, 490
bathmen, grain traders, the carpentering, lyre-pegging,
  shield-fastening crowd.
In the dark men put on their shoes and set forth—

Euelpides
                                                                I'll vouch for that!
I lost a coat of Phrygian wool, poor bastard, thanks to him.
I'd been invited to the city for a child's naming day,
and had a bit to drink and a nap, when right before dinner   495
that bird up and crowed. I thought it was morning and leave for
  Halimus.
I leave the city walls and a mugger saps me with a club.
I fall down, and before I can yell, he's already extracted my coat!

Peisetaerus
To resume: back then the kite was the ruler and king over Greece.

Chorus Leader
Over Greece?

Peisetaerus
                        That's right, and as king he instituted the custom   500
of rolling on the ground before kites.°

Euelpides
                                          Yes, I rolled with the rest
when I saw a kite, and when I was on my back with my mouth open
I swallowed an obol,° so I had to lug my sack home empty.

Peisetaerus
What's more, the cuckoo was king of all Egypt and Phoenicia;
and whenever the cuckoo said "cuckoo," all the Phoenicians   505
would start reaping the wheat and barley in their fields.

Euelpides
So that's what that saying means, "Cuckoo! Knobs out and up
  country!"°

---

501 At their first appearance each year, as being harbingers of spring.
503 Lacking pockets, Athenians carried small coins in their mouths.
507 Perhaps a reveille call meaning "arise and prepare to march;" "knobs" translates
       psoloi, a word referring to men with foreskins exposed (suggesting erection in the
       case of Greeks, who did not practice circumcision; and circumcision in the case of
       barbarians, who did).

Peisetaerus

And so dominant was their dominion that in the Greek cities
if some Agamemnon or Menelaus ever *was* king,
a bird would be perched on his sceptre, getting a share of
   his presents. 510

Euelpides

You know, that's something I never realized. I was always bewildered
when in the tragedies someone like Priam came on with a bird, but of
   course
it was perched there to watch what presents Lysicrates° pocketed.

Peisetaerus

But the absolute clincher is that Zeus, the current king,
stands with an eagle on his head as an emblem of royalty, 515
as does his daughter° with an owl, and Apollo, *qua* servant, with a
   hawk.

Chorus Leader

By Demeter, that's absolutely right—but why have they got them?

Peisetaerus

Well, when a sacrificer puts guts into the god's hand, as is customary,
why, the birds themselves can grab the guts before Zeus can!
And in those days nobody'd swear by a god; they all swore
   by birds. 520
Even today Lampon° swears "by Goose" when he's pulling a scam.
That's how high and holy everyone deemed you then;
but now you're mere knaves, simpletons, tomfools!
These days they pelt you like lunatics;
and even in the temples 525
every bird-hunter's out to get you,
setting nooses, snares, limed twigs,
toils, meshes, nets, decoys in traps.
And when they catch you they sell you wholesale,
and the customers get to feel you up. 530
And if they do buy you, they're not content
to have you roasted and served up;
no, they grate on cheese, oil,
silphium, vinegar, and they whip up
a second sauce, sweet and shiny, 535

---

513 Evidently an office holder or politician; the name is not uncommon.
516 Athena.
521 A distinguished authority on oracles and religious protocol, and prominent in public
   life since the 440s; ridiculed elsewhere in comedy for high living.

and baste it on hot,
when you're hot yourselves,
like meat from carcasses!

Chorus (antistrophe)

Very harrowing, yes very, is the tale
you've brought us, human. It made me weep   540
at my fathers' baseness,
who in my own time have wrecked these privileges of mine
that my forebears bequeathed to them.
But now you're here, by the grace of god or some happy chance,
to be my savior.   545
So shall I live, entrusting to you
my nestlings and myself.

Chorus Leader

Now instruct us what we should do, because our life won't be
worth living, unless at all costs we recover our sovereignty.

Peisetaerus

Then I instruct you first to make a single city of birds;   550
then encircle the whole atmosphere, all the area between
the earth and sky, with a wall of big baked bricks, like Babylon.

Chorus Leader

Cebriones and Porphyrion,° what a redoubtable citadel!

Peisetaerus

And when that's up and ready, reclaim your rulership from Zeus;
if he refuses, and isn't willing, and doesn't give up at once,   555
declare a holy war against him, and deny the gods
the right to travel through your territory with erections,
the way they used to descend for adultery with their Alcmenes°
and Alopes° and Semeles.° And if they do trespass,
then clap a seal on their boners, so they can't fuck any more
   women.   560
And I urge you to despatch another bird as a herald to mankind,
to say that, the birds being sovereign, they must henceforth sacrifice
to the birds, and only afterwards to the gods; and that they must aptly
assign to each of the gods the bird who's a fitting counterpart:
if the offering's to Aphrodite, offer nuts to the phall-arope bird;   565
if the offering's a sheep to Poseidon, consecrate granola to the duck;

---

553 Two of the Giants, whose rebellion against the Olympian gods was crushed in the
    Plain of Phlegra (cf. lines 824-25); porphyrion was also the name of a bird.
558 Alcmene, Amphitryon's wife, was mother by Zeus of Heracles.
559 Alope, Cercyon's daughter, was mother by Poseidon of Hippothoon.
559 Semele, Cadmus' daughter, was mother by Zeus of Dionysus.

if something's to be offered to Heracles, offer honeypies to the cormo-
rant;
and if it's a ram for Zeus the King, the nuthatch is a king bird,°
and it's to him, not Zeus, that a gnat with intact nuts must be slaughtered.

Euelpides

I like that, slaughtering a gnat! So let the great Zan° thunder away! 570

Chorus Leader

But how are humans supposed to believe we're gods and not daws?
We fly and have wings.

Peisetaerus

That's nonsense! Why, Hermes certainly flies
and wears wings, and he's a god, and so do a great many other gods;
Victory, for one, flies on golden wings, and so does Cupid,
and according to Homer Iris is "like to a trembling dove."° 575

Euelpides

And won't Zeus thunder at us and hurl his "wingéd lightning bolt"?

Peisetaerus

But if out of ignorance they still consider you nothing
and consider the Olympians gods, then a cloud of sparrows
and seed pickers must arise and gobble up their seed in the fields.
Then when they're famished, let Demeter° dole out grain to them! 580

Euelpides

She'll renege, by Zeus; mark my words, she'll just make excuses.°

Peisetaerus

And the ravens should peck out the eyes of the oxen harnessed
to plough their land, and of their sheep, as a challenge.
Then let Apollo the Healer heal them—and earn his fee!

Euelpides

Please, wait at least until I've sold my own pair of oxen! 585

Peisetaerus

But if they accept you as god, as Zeus, as Earth, as Cronus, as
Poseidon,
then all good things will be theirs.

---

568 It is unclear what bird *orchilos* refers to (perhaps the wren), and why it was a "king"
bird (perhaps a reference to the wren's gold crown or to Aesop's fable 434); the translation preserves the pun on *orcheis* "testicles."
570 A cultic form of Zeus' name.
575 *Homeric Hymn to Apollo* 114.
580 Demeter ("Mother Earth"), the Roman Ceres, was the goddess responsible for the
fertility of crops, especially cereal grains.
581 As comic poets alleged of populist politicians.

Chorus Leader
What good things, for example?

Peisetaerus
For starters, the locusts won't devour their vine blooms;
a single contingent of owls and kestrels will wipe them out.
Then again, the mites and the gallflies won't always devour their fig
trees;   590
a single flock of thrushes will eat them all clean up.

Chorus Leader
But how will we give them wealth? Because that's their principal
passion.

Peisetaerus
When they practice augury these birds will give them the
motherlodes,
and to the diviner they'll reveal the profitable voyages,
so that no shipowner will be lost.

Chorus Leader
Won't be lost? How so?   595

Peisetaerus
When he asks the diviner about a voyage, a bird will tip him:
"Don't sail, a storm's on its way;" "Sail now, you'll make a profit."

Euelpides
I'm buying a ship and taking on cargo—not staying with you guys!

Peisetaerus
And they'll show them the hoards of silver that the old-timers buried;
these birds know where they lie. You do hear everyone say,   600
"No one but maybe some bird knows where *my* treasure lies."

Euelpides
I'm selling that ship, getting a shovel, and digging up pots!

Chorus Leader
But how will birds give them health? That rests with the gods.

Peisetaerus
If they're wealthy, they're plenty healthy, no?

Euelpides
You know it!
No human's healthy at all if he's doing poorly.   605

Chorus Leader
But how will they reach old age? That's also up to Olympus.
Or must they die when they're tykes?

Peisetaerus
> Heavens no, the birds will add
> an extra 300 years to their lives.

Chorus Leader
> Where from?

Peisetaerus
> Why, from themselves:
> don't you know that "five ages of man lives the croaking crow"?°

Euelpides
> Well dammit, these birds are far better kings for us than Zeus!   610

Peisetaerus
> Far better for sure!
> To begin with, we needn't
> build them marble temples
> and gild the gates with gold;
> they'll make their homes   615
> in copses and woods,
> while for the bird VIPs an olive tree
> will be their temple.
> And we'll not be going to Delphi or Ammon°
> and sacrificing there; instead we'll stand   620
> among strawberries and wild olives
> holding grains of barley and wheat
> in our outstretched hands,
> and pray to them to give us a share of blessings;
> and we'll get these blessings right away,   625
> just for tossing them some grains of wheat!

LYRIC SCENE
(Chorus Leader, Chorus, Peisetaerus, Tereus, Euelpides, Procne)

Chorus Leader
> Old man, my worst foe changed to my very best friend,
> there's no way I could ever choose to discard this idea of yours!

Chorus
> Emboldened by your words,
> I give notice and solemnly swear: 630
> if you bring to my cause congenial proposals,
> and fairly, squarely, righteously attack the gods,

---

609 From a lost work of Hesiod, fragment 304.
619 A ram-headed Egyptian god, identified by the Greeks with Zeus, who had an oracular shrine at the Siwa oasis in Libya.

tuning your thoughts to mine, then not much longer
will the gods be abusing my sceptre!

Chorus Leader
　So in the tasks that call for brawn, we're ready for duty;　　　　635
　in the plans that call for brains, you be in charge of all that.

Peisetaerus
　Well then, there's absolutely no time left for napping
　or a spell of Nicias' Paralysis;°
　no, we've got to accomplish something, and fast!

Tereus
　　But first　　　　640
　do come along inside, come into my nest,
　that is, such sticks and twigs as I call home,
　and both of you tell us your names.

Peisetaerus
　　That's easy enough:
　my name is Peisetaerus, and this one here
　is Euelpides of Crioa.°

Tereus
　　A hearty welcome　　　　645
　to you both!

Peisetaerus
　We thank you.

Tereus
　Well then, do come in.

Peisetaerus
　Well, let's go in. Please, show us in.

Tereus
　Come on, then!

Peisetaerus
　But, um, hold on, reverse oars back this way!
　Look here, please tell us, how can my pal and I
　be your partners when you all can fly but we can't?　　　　650

Tereus
　Just fine.

---

638 Nicias had urged caution in sending the armada against Sicily (Thucydides 6.8, 25), and then had failed to follow up his victory before Syracuse (6.71).
644 For the significance of the names see 1-2 nn. Crioa was an actual Attic deme, but the comic point is unclear.

Peisetaerus
Mind you now, there's a story in Aesop's fables
concerning the fox, how once upon a time
she fared very poorly in partnership with an eagle.°

Tereus
Never fear, I know of a certain little root;
just chew it and you'll get a pair of wings.   655

Peisetaerus
It's a deal; let's go inside. Come on then, Xanthias
and Manodorus, pick up the baggage there.

Chorus Leader
Yoo hoo! Yes you. A word, please.

Tereus
What's the matter?

Chorus Leader
Take these men
and lunch them well; but that mellifluous nightingale, the Muses'
chorister,
bring her out here and leave her with us; we'd like to play
with her.   660

Peisetaerus
Oh yes, by all means do just what they ask!
Bring the chick out here, out of the tickle grass.

Euelpides
My heavens yes, do bring her out; we'd like
to have a look at the nightingale ourselves.

Tereus
Well, if that's what you both want, I must oblige.
Oh Procne! Come out and say hello to our guests.   665

Peisetaerus
Good god almighty, what a beautiful chick!
So tender and fair!

Euelpides
                    Know what I'd like to do?
I'd really like to spread those drumsticks of hers!

---

653 The fable (Aesop 1, first attested in Archilochus fragments 172-81) tells how the eagle
  had betrayed the fox by feeding her cubs to its eaglets, and the flightless fox could
  only curse the eagle; but when the eagle took hot goat-meat from an altar she set her
  nest afire, and the fox ate the eaglets as they fell.

Peisetaerus
She's got quite a choker, like a debutante! 670

Euelpides
Me, I think I'd also like to kiss her.

Peisetaerus
Look, you screw-up, her beak's a pair of skewers!

Euelpides
OK, it's like an egg: we'll just have to peel
that shell off her head and kiss her thataway!

Tereus
Let's go inside.

Peisetaerus
Lead the way, and good luck to us! 675

PARABASIS°
(Chorus, Chorus Leader)

Chorus
Ah darling warbler,
ah, dearest of birds,
songmate of all my hymns,
my nightingale companion,
you're here, you're here, you're manifest , 680
bringing sweet sound to me.
Now, weaver of springtime tunes
on the fair-toned pipes,
lead off our anapests.

---

676 The *parabasis* ("self-revelation") of the chorus is a standard feature of Old Comedy
that allowed the poet, through speeches by the chorus-leader, to address, and also to
admonish, the spectators about any issues he cared to raise, whether or not they
were directly relevant to the issues raised in the rest of the play. The parabasis of
Birds is unusual in that the Chorus Leader stays in dramatic character rather than
speaking on the poet's behalf, and does not comment on any topic of current political
or social interest. Instead, on the birds' behalf, he produces a systematic cosmogony
in response to Peisetaerus' earlier revelation that they had once been all-powerful
gods (the cosmogony is based mainly on Hesiod's *Theogony*, but with an admixture
of other cosmogonic and pseudo-scientific poetry); and then he invites the spectators
to taste the liberty and advantages associated with having wings.
  The structure of this parabasis is (1) the parabasis proper (a speech by the Chorus
Leader, often—as here—called "the anapests" after its characteristic rhythm), followed by (2) an "epirrhematic syzygy" consisting of an *ode* (a paired, or responsional,
song) and an *epirrheme* (a paired, or responsional, speech) followed by their
responsional *antode* and *antepirrheme*. The epirrhematic syzygy is so called because
its *epirrhemes* are "yoked together" by songs in an ABAB pattern. *Birds*, like some of
Aristophanes' other plays, has a second parabasis (lines 1058-1117) consisting only
of the epirrhematic syzygy.

Chorus Leader
Ye men by nature just faintly alive, like the race of leaves,   685
ye do-littles, artefacts of clay, tribes shadowy and feeble,
ye wingless ephemerals, suffering mortals, dreamlike people:
now pay ye attention to us, the immortals, the gods everlasting,
the etherial, the ageless, whose counsels are imperishable;
once you hear from us the truth about all celestial phenomena,   690
and the true nature of birds, the genesis of gods, rivers, Erebus, and
      Chaos,°
then you'll be able to tell Prodicus from me to go to hell!°
In the beginning were Chaos and Night and black Erebus and
broad Tartarus,°
no Earth, no Air nor Sky. But in the boundless bosom of Erebus
did black-winged Night at the very start bring forth a wind-egg,°   695
from which as the seasons revolved came forth Eros the seductive,
like a swift-wheeling whirlwind, his back aglitter with wings of gold.
And mating by night with winged Chaos in broad Tartarus,
he hatched our very own race and first brought us up to the daylight.
No race of immortal gods till Eros commingled everything;   700
then, this commingling with that, Sky came to be, and Ocean
and Earth, and'the whole imperishable race of blessed gods.
Thus *we're* far older than the blessed gods; it's abundantly clear
that we're Eros' offspring: we fly and consort with lovers. Yes,
many fair boys swear they won't, and almost make it to the end   705
of their bloom, but thanks to *our* power their lovers do spread their
      thighs,
one presenting a quail, another a porphyrion, a goose, or a Persian
      bird.
And from us, the birds, do mortals get all their greatest blessings.
To start with, we reveal the seasons of spring, winter, and autumn.
It's time to sow when the crane whoops off to Africa;   710
that's when it tells the shipowner to hang up his rudder and rest,
and Orestes° to weave a cloak so he won't catch cold as he mugs you.
And then it's the kite's turn to appear and reveal a new season,
when it's time to shear the sheep's spring wool. And then there's the
      swallow,

---

691 Two of Hesiod's primeval entities ("Darkness" and "Void").
692 Prodicus of Ceos, a contemporary of Socrates with broad scientific and philosophical
      interests, traced the origin of gods to primitive nature- and hero-worship.
693 The darkest region of the underworld.
695 It was thought that some birds could be impregnated by the wind, producing
      unhatchable eggs.
712 The nickname of the son of one Timocrates, after the mythical hero who wandered
      insane to Athens after killing his own mother.

and now you ought to sell your coat and buy a jacket. 715
And we're your Ammon,° Delphi,° Dodona,° and Phoebus Apollo,
for you embark on nothing without first consulting the birds,
whether it's business, or making a living, or a man who's getting
   married.
Whatever's decisive in prophecy you deem a bird:
to you, an ominous word's a bird, a sneeze is a bird, 720
a chance meeting, a sound, a good-luck servant, a donkey: all birds.
So isn't it obvious that we're your prophetic Apollo?
Well then, if you treat us as gods,
you'll have your prophets, muses,
breezes, seasons, winter, 725
mild summer, stifling heat. And we won't run off
and sit up there preening
among the clouds, like Zeus,
but ever at hand we'll bestow on you,
your children, and your children's children 730
healthy wealthiness,
happiness, prosperity, peace,
youth, hilarity, dances, festivities,
and birds' milk. Why, you're liable
to knock yourself out from good living, 735
that's how rich you'll all be!

Chorus (strophe)
Bosky Muse—
tio tio tio tio tinx!—
of intricate tone, joining you
mid the vales and mountain peaks,— 740
tio tio tio tio tinx!—
perched on a leaf-tressed ash,—
tio tio tio tio tinx!—
from my vibrant throat I pour forth
sacred strains of song for Pan 745
and holy dance tunes for the Mountain Mother°—
to to to to to to to to to tinx!—
whence like a bee

---

716 See 619 n.
716 The chief oracular shrine of the Greeks, sacred to Phoebus Apollo, and also con-
    sulted by other peoples.
716 In Epirus, in NW Greece, where Zeus had an oracle.
746 Cybele, the Anatolian mother-goddess; both she and Pan (a god of wild mountains
    and forests) were worshipped at Athens.

Phrynichus° ever sipped the nectar
of ambrosial music   750
to bring forth his sweet song—
tio tio tio tio tinx!

Chorus Leader
Spectators, if any of you out there wants to sew up the rest
of your life quite pleasantly with the birds, come here to us.
Because whatever's shameful here, for people controlled by
    custom,   755
it's all considered admirable among us birds.
Is father-beating considered shameful by custom here?
Up there it's perfectly admirable to rush your father,
hit him, and say "Put up your spur if you mean to fight!"
You happen to be a runaway slave with a branded forehead?   760
With us you'll be simply be called a dappled francolin!
You happen to be no less a Phrygian than Spintharus?°
Up here you'll be a pigeon of Philemon's° breed!
Even if you're a slave and a Carian like Execestides,°
join us, sprout some forefeathers, and presto, proper kinfolk!   765
And if Peisias' son wants to betray the gates to the outlaws,
let him become a partridge, a chick of the old cock, since among us
there's nothing shameful in playing partridge tricks.°

Chorus (antistrophe) °
Just so did swans—
tio tio tio tio tinx!—   770
beating wings in unison
raise a harmonious whoop for Apollo—
tio tio tio tio tinx!—
gathered on the bank by Hebrus River—
tio tio tio tio tinx!   775
their whooping pierced the cloud of heaven;

---

749 The songs of this tragic poet, an older contemporary of Aeschylus, were still popular
    among the older generation of Athenians.
762 Phrygians at Athens would be slaves; the Spintharus teased here for foreign ancestry
    may be the father of the fourth-century statesman Eubulus.
763 Unknown; the point is that Athenians without family connections will be pedigreed
    birds.
764 See 11 n.
768 Peisias' son was perhaps the Cleombrotus elsewhere called "son of Partridge" (cf.
    1292-93); "the outlaws" are probably those denounced in the sacrileges of 415, who
    had fled Athens and were condemned *in absentia*; "tricks" refers to the partridge's
    skill at evading pursuers.
768 This song probably recollects Apollo's journey from the Hyperboreans to Delphi in a
    swan-drawn chariot, which Alcaeus had described in a famous paean (fragment 307).

the manifold tribes of beasts were cowed,
and the cloudless clear air quenched the waves—
to to to to to to to to to tinx!—
All Olympus reverberated,   780
amazement seized its lords, and the Olympian
Graces and Muses
replied in cheerful song—
tio tio tio tio tinx!

Chorus Leader
There's nothing better or merrier than sprouting wings.   785
Say one of you spectators had a pair of wings,
and got hungry, and grew bored with the tragic performances;
then *he'd* have flown out of here, gone home, had lunch,
and when he was full, flown back here again to see us.
And if some Patrocleides° out there had to shit,   790
he wouldn't have fouled his cloak; no, he'd have flown off,
blown a fart, caught his breath, and flown right back again.
And if anyone out there happens to be an adulterer,
and sees the lady's husband in the Councillors' seats,°
he'd have used his wings to launch himself out of here,   795
and gone and fucked her, and then flown back again.
So isn't getting wings worth any price?
Dieitrephes,° with only chianti-bottle wings,°
was elected chief, then captain: starting from nothing,
then flying high, an actual zooming horsecock.°   800

EPISODE
(Peisetaerus, Euelpides, Chorus Leader, Xanthias, Manes)

Peisetaerus
Ta da, here we are! My God, I can't recall
my ever having seen a funnier sight!

Euelpides
What are *you* laughing at?

---

790 The proposer of two decrees, otherwise unknown.
794 The 500 members of the Council had a block of reserved seats up front.
798 Despite his comic caricature as a distasteful arriviste, Dieitrephes' family was in fact
distinguished. In his current generalship he would command the Thracians responsible for the massacre at Mycalessus described by Thucydides 7.29-30, and later he
would later become an oligarch (8.64).
798 As the wicker handles were called.
800 A mythical beast often depicted by Attic painters of the 6th and early 5th c. and
mentioned by Aeschylus in his lost play, *Myrmidons* (fragment 134), used of strutting
officers.

Peisetaerus
Those wing-feathers of yours.
Do you know what you look just like in those wings?
A painting of a goose made for the thriftshop!   805

Euelpides
And you look like a blackbird with a bowl cut!

Peisetaerus
As Aeschylus said, we're stuck with these comparisons
"not at others' hands but by our very own feathers."°

Chorus Leader
Now, what's on our agenda?

Peisetaerus
First, we should give
our city a name, something grand and notable;   810
then sacrifice to the gods.

Euelpides
My sentiments exactly.

Chorus Leader
Let's see then, what name will our city have?

Peisetaerus
What do you say we give it that impressive name
from Lacedaemonia, Sparta?

Euelpides
Great Heracles,
do you think I'd stick *my* city with a name like Sparta?°   815
Not even for a mattress°—if I had nice wide slats instead.

Peisetaerus
Then what name *will* we give it?

Chorus Leader
A name suggesting
all this, the clouds and aerial spaces; something
very highfalutin.

Peisetaerus
How about Cloudcuckooland?

---

807 *Myrmidons* fragment 139, where Achilles, blaming himself for Patroclus' death, recalls an eagle shot by an arrow fletched with eagle feathers.
815 Sparta was Athens' main antagonist in the Peloponnesian War.
816 Punning on "esparto" twine.

Chorus Leader
Yes, yes!
You've found an absolutely great and wonderful name!   820

Euelpides
Sure, this must be the same Cloudcuckooland
where most of Theogenes'° assets are,
and all of Aeschines'.°

Peisetaerus
                              No, even better than that:
it's the Plain of Phlegra, where the very Gods
outshot the Children of Earth at empty bragging!°   825

Chorus Leader
A gleaming° great city! Now what god shall be
the Citadel Guardian? For whom shall we weave the Robe?°

Peisetaerus
Why not let Athena Polias have the job?

Euelpides
But how can a city remain well disciplined,
where a god born a woman stands there wearing armor,   830
while a Cleisthenes° sits there with a sewing kit?

Chorus Leader
Then who *will* be taking charge of the city's Storkade?°

Peisetaerus
One of our birds, a bird of the Persian breed,°
the one universally known as a very fearsome
Chick of Ares.

Euelpides
    My Lord and Master Chick!   835
And that's a god so well suited to life on the rocks.

Peisetaerus
Come on now, Euelpides, you take off for the sky

---

821 A common name, here perhaps the Theogenes ridiculed elsewhere for imaginary
      wealth.
822 Ridiculed as a boaster elsewhere.
825 See 553 n.
826 A favorite epithet of Athens.
827 Athena Polias ("of the Citadel") was Citadel Guardian of Athens, and every four
      years was presented with a robe at the festival of the Great Panathenaea.
831 Often ridiculed as a beardless effeminate.
832 The *Pelargikon* (~ *pelargos* "stork"), designated the Mycenaean walls of the Acropolis
      and an enclosure at its foot.
833 See 483-84.

and make yourself useful to the builders of our walls:
take them up gravel, roll up your sleeves and mix some mortar,
hand up a trough, fall off the scaffolding,   840
station site watchmen, keep the embers glowing,
run a tour with the bell, and bed down right on site.
Now send one herald up to the gods above,
and another herald down to mankind below,
and then report to me.

Euelpides

And you can stay   845
and report to me—in hell!

Peisetaerus

Friend, do as I say;
none of what I've talked about can be done without you.
As for me, I'd better sacrifice to the new gods,
so I'll invite the priest to organize the procession.
Slave! Slave! Pick up the basket and the holy water.   850

Chorus (strophe)
I am with you, I concur,
I hereby endorse your advice
to approach the gods
with grand and solemn hymns
as we curry their favor as well   855
by sacrificing a wee sheep.
Up up up with a Pythian cry,
and let Chaeris pipe as we sing.°

EPISODE
(Peisetaerus, Priest)

Peisetaerus
Now stop that piping! Heracles, what *is* this?
By god, I've seen a lot of amazing sights,   860
but this I've never seen, a raven playing the pipes!
Well, Priest, you're on; start sacrificing to the new gods.

Priest
I certainly will, but where's the boy with the basket?   863
All pray:° to Hestia of the Birds, to Kite their Hearthkeeper, to the
     Olympian birds and birdesses each and all—

---

858 A lyre player and piper often ridiculed in comedy for poor technique.
864 The Priest's invocations in lines 864-88 are in prose.

Peisetaerus
Hail, Hawk of Sunium,° Lord of the Seastork!   865

Priest
and the Swan of Pytho and Delos,° and Leto the Quail Mother,° and
Artemis the Curlew—

Peisetaerus
No more Colaenis,° now it's Artemis Curlew!   872

Priest
and Pigeon Sabazius,° and the Great Ostrich Mother of gods and
men°—

Peisetaerus
Lady Cybele the Ostrich, mother of Cleocritus!°   876

Priest
grant to the inhabitants of Cloudcuckooland health and security, and
for the Chians as well—°

Peisetaerus
It's funny how the Chians get tacked on everywhere!   880

Priest
and the Avian heroes and the Heroes' children, Porphyrion and White
Pelican and Grey Pelican and Red Hawk and Grouse and Peacock
and Reed Warbler and Teal and Harrier and Heron and Tern and
Black Tit and Blue Tit—   888

Peisetaerus
Stop, damn you, stop your invitations! Whew!
How big do you think this victim is, you jinx,   890
that you're inviting eagles and vultures to share?
A single kite could snatch the whole thing away.
Now get out of here, and take your wreaths with you!
I'll perform this sacrifice here all by myself.

Chorus (antistrophe)
Then once more in your service   895
I will raise a second song,
godfearing and pious,

---

865 A promontory on the SE tip of Attica, where Poseidon had a temple.
866 The sacred bird of Apollo.
866 I.e. the corncrake, alluding to Ortygia (Quail Island), where Leto gave birth to Artemis.
872 Artemis' cult title in the Attic deme Myrrhinus.
873 A Phrygian god associated with Dionysus and popular with women and slaves.
873 Like Cybele, the Great Mother, the Great Ostrich (now extinct) was from Asia.
876 Not certainly identifiable.
877 In the Athenian empire Chios and Methymna enjoyed the special status of autonomous allies.

for the ablution,
and invite the blessed gods—
just one of them, 900
if you all want to have enough meat;
for the sacrifice you've got there is nothing
but a goatee and horns.

EPISODE
(Poet, Peisetaerus, Oracle Collector, Meton, Inspector, Decree Seller)

Poet
"Cloudcuckooland
the Blest now celebrate, 905
O Muse, in your hymns of song!"

Peisetaerus
Now where did he come from? Please identify yourself.

Poet
"I am he that launches a song of honey-tongued verses,
the Muses' eager vassal,"
to quote Homer. 910

Peisetaerus
Don't tell me you're a slave, wearing hair that long?

Poet
"No, we master singers all
are the Muses' eager vassals,"
to quote Homer.

Peisetaerus
Then no wonder you've got a meager jacket, too! 915
Now why the hell did you come up here, poet?

Poet
I've written songs for your Cloudcuckooland,
yes, lots of beautiful dithyrambs,° and songs
for maidens, and songs à la Simonides.°

Peisetaerus
Just when did you start to write these songs? From when? 920

Poet
I've been celebrating this city for a long, long time.

---

918 Choral performances honoring Dionysus; at the Athenian Dionysia there was a tribally sponsored contest for choruses of boys and of old men.
919 Simonides of Ceos (*c.* 566-468), reputedly the first poet to compose for a fee, had an ancient reputation for avarice.

Peisetaerus
But I've just begun its tenth-day sacrifice,
and just named it, like a baby, moments ago!

Poet
"Nay, the Muses' voice is a swift one,
like the twinkle of horses' hooves.   925
But you, father, founder of Aetna,
namesake of holy rites,
grant me whatever you wish
by your nod
graciously to grant."°   930

Peisetaerus
This pest is going to cause us lots of trouble
unless we give him something, and thus give him the slip.
You there, you've got a shirt on and a vest;
take them off and give them to our artful poet.
Here, take this vest; you seem to me quite frigid.   935

Poet
"With no reluctance does my dear
Muse accept this gift;
but learn you in your heart
a Pindaric saying—"°

Peisetaerus
The fellow just won't take his leave of us!   940

Poet
"Yea among Scythian nomads does wander
apart from his people
the one who possesses no shuttle-actuated raiment;
and inglorious does go a jerkin without a jacket.
Pray understand what I mean."   945

Peisetaerus
I understand that you want to snag that jacket.
Take it off; we've got to help the poet out.
Now take this here, and off you go.

Poet
                                   I'm off;
when I get home I'll write this for your city:
"Celebrate, Muse on golden throne, the shivering, freezing land;   950

---

930 Adapting a poem by Pindar (fragment 105a) for the Syracusan ruler Hieron, who
    founded Aetna in 476/5.
939 Pindar fragment 105b.

to the snowblown
many-pathed plains have I come."
Hurrah!

Peisetaerus
But surely you've escaped from the freezing cold,
now that you've snagged that little jacket there!   955
Good god, that was a hassle I never expected,
that he should have heard about our city so soon.
Boy, make another circuit with that holy water.
Auspicious speech, please.

Oracle Collector°
                    Don't start on that goat!

Peisetaerus
What? Who are you?

Oracle Collector
                    Why, an oracle collector.

Peisetaerus
                                        Then to hell with you.   960

Oracle Collector
Good heavens, you mustn't make light of religious matters!
There is an oracle of Bacis° referring explicitly
to Cloudcuckooland.

Peisetaerus
                    Then how comes it that
you didn't divulge this oracle before I founded
this city?

Oracle Collector
    Religious scruple held me back.   965

Peisetaerus
Well, nothing beats listening to the actual verses.

Oracle Collector
"Nay when wolves and grey crows shall together have their abode
in the place twixt Corinth and Sicyon—"°

Peisetaerus
Look here, what have I got to do with any Corinthians?°

---

957 A person with a collection of purportedly venerable oracles, which for a fee he could
       use to interpret current, or predict future, events.
962 A legendary prophet whose oracles, many of which concerned international rela-
       tions, were collected and discussed during the Peloponnesian War.
968 Riddling, because these territories were contiguous.
969 Athens and Corinth had long been bitter enemies.

Oracle Collector
By that enigma Bacis meant the sky.   970
"first sacrifice to Pandora° a ram with snowy fleece,
and whosoever arrives first as expounder of my words,
to him give a spotless cloak and fresh sandals—" .

Peisetaerus
Are sandals really in there?

Oracle Collector
                                Here's the book.
"and give him the chalice, and fill up his hands with innards—"   975

Peisetaerus
Is giving innards in there too?

Oracle Collector
    Here's the book.
"and if, inspired youth, you carry out the orders I give you,
you shall become an eagle midst the clouds; but if you give not,
you shall be not a turtledove, not a rock thrush, not a woodpecker."

Peisetaerus
Is all that really in there?

Oracle Collector
                                Here's the book.   980

Peisetaerus
Well now, your oracle doesn't at all match *this* one,
which I personally wrote down from Apollo:
"Yea when a charlatan type who arrives uninvited
vexes the sacrificers and desires a share of the innards,
then must you smite him in the place twixt the ribs—"   985

Oracle Collector
I think you must be kidding.

Peisetaerus
                                Here's the book.
"and spare not even an eagle midst the clouds,
not if he be Lampon nor yet the great Diopeithes."°

Oracle Collector
Is all that really in there?

---

971 Not the allegorical girl with the jar of evils in Hesiod's *Works* 42-105, but the earth
   goddess whose name means "giver of all gifts," some of which the Oracle Collector
   now hopes to receive.
987 Both were famous oracular experts, and the latter a prosecutor of atheists and intel-
   lectuals.

Peisetaerus
Here's the book!
Now get the hell out of here!

Oracle Collector
Oh mercy me!   990

Peisetaerus
Go on, scat! Oracle monger somewhere else!

Meton°
I have come here to you—

Peisetaerus
Here's another nuisance.
You've come here to do what? What form does your plan take?
What idea, what buskin, is afoot?

Meton
I want to do a survey of the air   995
for you, and parcel it into acres.

Peisetaerus
For heaven's sake,
who on earth are you?

Meton
Who am I? Why, Meton,
renowned in Greece, and in Colonus too.°

Peisetaerus
And pray tell what's all this you've got?

Meton
Air rulers.
Because for starters, the sky in its entirety   1000
is like a casserole cover. Accordingly,
I'll position this ruler, which is curved, along the top,
inserting a compass—you follow?

Peisetaerus
No, I don't.

Meton
—and lay a straight ruler alongside, take a measure,
so you'll get a circle squared, with a marketplace   1005
in the center, with streets running straight into it there

---

992 The famous geometer and astronomer. His unmanly caricature in this scene may be
   connected with the rumor that he had resorted to arson just before the expedition to
   Sicily in order to evade service.
997 A district of downtown Athens where Meton had set up a sundial.

and meeting at the very center, as from a star,
itself being round, straight rays will beam on out
in every direction.

Peisetaerus

The man's a Thales.°
Meton—

Meton

What is it?

Peisetaerus

You know I'm fond of you,   1010
so do take my advice and hit the road.

Meton
What's the problem?

Peisetaerus

As in Sparta they're expelling
all foreigners, and punches have started to fly
pretty thick and fast all over.

Meton

It's civil war?

Peisetaerus
God no, not that!

Meton

What then?

Peisetaerus

There's a unanimous   1015
decision to beat up all the charlatans.

Meton
Then I *will* be going.

Peisetaerus

That's smart; but you might not
get away in time: those punches are close at hand!

Meton
Heaven help me!

Peisetaerus

Didn't I try to warn you?
Go somewhere else, and then survey yourself!   1020

1007 The early sixth century founder of the Milesian school of natural science and phi-
losophy, who had become a byword for genius.

Inspector°
Where can I find consuls?

Peisetaerus
Who's this Sardanapallus?°

Inspector
I'm an Inspector, duly allotted to come here
and visit Cloudcuckooland.

Peisetaerus
Inspector, eh?
On whose authority?

Inspector
Some petty bill
of Teleas's.°

Peisetaerus
Then what say you just take   1025
your pay and leave, without any fuss?

Inspector
God yes,
I will. I should be back home at the Assembly anyway;
there's some business I've been handling for Pharnaces.°

Peisetaerus
Take your pay and leave; I've got it right here   in my fist!

Inspector
Hey, what was that?

Peisetaerus
An assembly about Pharnaces.   1030

Inspector
Witnesses! Inspector under attack!

Peisetaerus
Shoo, away with you, and your ballot boxes too!
Amazing—they're already sending inspectors to our city,
before we've even held our founding sacrifice!

Decree Seller
"And if a Cloudcuckoolander offends against an Athenian—"   1035

1020 Exemplifying the travelling inspectors sent by Assembly decree to enforce Athenian
    policies in the cities of the empire.
1021 According to the Greeks, the wealthy and degenerate last king of Assyria before the
    loss of that empire to the Medes and Babylonians in the late seventh century.
1024 See 168 n.
1027 A Persian satrap.

Peisetaerus
What sort of nuisance is this now, that book there?

Decree Seller
A decree seller, that's me, and I've travelled here
to sell you some brand new laws.

Peisetaerus
What sort of laws?

Decree Seller
"The Cloudcuckoolanders are to use the selfsame measures,   1040
weights, and decrees as the Olophyxians."°

Peisetaerus
And *you'll* soon be getting the same as the Black-and-Bluesians!

Decree Seller
Hey, what's the matter with you?

Peisetaerus
Away with your laws!
In a moment I'll be showing you some hurtful laws!   1045

Inspector
I summon Peisetaerus to appear
in the month of Munychion on a charge of assault!

Peisetaerus
Oh, is that right? What are *you* still doing here?

Decree Seller
"And should anyone expel the officials and refuse them entry under
the terms of the decree—"   1050

Peisetaerus
Oh heaven help me, are *you* still hereabouts too?

Inspector
I'll *ruin* you! I'll write you up for a ten thousand drachma—

Peisetaerus
And I'll smash both of your ballot boxes!

Decree Seller
Recall those evenings you crapped on the inscribed decree?

Peisetaerus
Pew! Somebody grab him! Why don't you stick around?   1055
Let's get away from here as fast as we can,
inside, where we can sacrifice the goat to the gods.

1041 Parodying the language of the Coinage Decree (date uncertain), and substituting
"decrees" for "coinage." Olophyxos was a small Athenian ally on the Athos penin-
sula, chosen for the sake of the following pun.

SECOND PARABASIS°
(Chorus, Chorus Leader)

Chorus (strophe)
To me, the omniscient
and omnipotent, shall all mortals
now sacrifice with pious prayers.   1060
For I keep watch over all the earth,
and keep safe the blooming crops
by slaying the brood of all species
of critters, who with omnivorous jaws
devour all that in soil sprouts from the pod   1065
and the fruit of the trees where they perch;
and I slay those who spoil fragrant gardens
with defilements most offensive;
and upon creepers and biters every one
from the force of my wing   1070
comes murderous destruction.

Chorus Leader
On this very day,° you know, we hear it again proclaimed
that whoever of you shall kill Diagoras the Melian°
shall get a talent; likewise whoever kills any long-dead tyrant.°
So now we want to make our own announcement right here: 1075
whoever of you kills Philocrates the Sparrovian°
shall get a talent, and four for bringing him in alive,
because he strings finches together and sells them for seven an obol;
and furthermore that he blows up thrushes for degrading display;
and crams the nostrils of blackbirds with their own feathers;   1080
and also captures pigeons, and keeps them all caged up,
and forces them to play decoy, tethered to a net.
Well, that's the announcement we wanted to make. And whoever
    keeps birds
caged up in the yard, we order you to let them go;   1085
if you disobey, you'll be captured by the birds,
and it will be your turn to play decoy on *our* turf.

1057 See 676 n.
1072 Presumably (but not demonstrably) the first day of the Dionysia festival.
1073 Dubbed "Diagoras of Quibbleton" and associated with Socrates, he was outlawed
    by Assembly decree for writings (now lost) critical of the Eleusinian Mysteries.
1074 Though the last Athenian tyrant had been expelled in 510, and there had been no real
    threat of a return to tyranny since the Persian Wars, the recent scandals surrounding
    Alcibiades had reawakened popular fears of antidemocratic plots.
1076 See 14 n.

Chorus (antistrophe)

Happy the race of feathered
birds, who in the winter
need wear no woolen cloaks;   1090
nor in summer's stifling heat
do the long rays roast us.
For I dwell among the flora
in the lap of flowery meadows,
when the sun-crazy cicada with voice divine   1095
in the noonday heat intones his shrill song;
and I winter in hollow caverns,
frolicking with mountain nymphs;
and in spring we graze on myrtle berries,
maidenly in their white florets,   1100
and the fruits of the Graces' garden.

Chorus Leader

We'd like to say a word to the judges about winning the prize,
namely all the benefits we'll bestow on them all if they vote for us,
so they'll get far better gifts than the ones that Paris got.°
So let's begin with the thing that every judge craves most: 1105
those owls from Laureum;° they'll never run out on you;
no, they'll move right into your house, and in your wallets
they'll build their nests and fledge a brood of small change.
On top of that, you'll live in houses that look like temples,
because we'll roof your houses over with eagle gables.   1110
And if you draw a nice little post, then want to do
some pilfering, we'll equip you with a sharp crowbar.
And if you go out for dinner, we'll send you off with a gizzard.
But vote against us, you'd better make some copper lids
to wear, like statues, for any who doesn't have a lid,   1115
whenever you're wearing a white suit, that's just when you'll pay
the piper, getting crapped on by all of the birds en masse.

EPISODE

(Peisetaerus, First Messenger, Chorus Leader, Second Messenger, Chorus)

Peisetaerus

Our sacrifice, dear birds, has been auspicious.
But how strange that no messenger is here from the wall,
to brief us on how things are going there.   1120

1104 Priam's son Alexander, better known as Paris, serving as the judge of a divine beauty
   contest, got the world's most attractive woman, Helen, as a bribe from Aphrodite for
   picking her over Hera (who offered power) and Athena (who offered wisdom).
1106 Coins made from silver mined at Laureum and bearing Athena's owl as an emblem.

Wait, here comes a runner, panting like an Olympian.

First Messenger
Whe whe where's, whe whe whe where's, whe whe whe where's,
whe whe where's Peisetaerus, the ruler?

Peisetaerus
                              Over here.

First Messenger
Your wall is all built up.

Peisetaerus
                    That's very good news!

First Messenger
A very fine and very impressive achievement;   1125
it's so wide on top, Proxenides of Braggarton°
and Theogenes could hitch two chariots up
to horses the size of the wooden one at Troy
and pass each other head-on!

Peisetaerus
    Heracles!

First Messenger
And as for its height—and I measured it myself—   1130
it's a hundred fathoms.

Peisetaerus
    Poseidon, that is high!
Who can have built it up as tall as that?

First Messenger
Birds and birds alone, with no Egyptian
brickbearer in sight, no mason, no carpenter,
but all with their own hands, an amazing sight to see.   1135
From Libya there came some thirty thousand,
cranes, who'd swallowed stones for the foundations,
and these the corncrakes blocked up with their bills,
while another ten thousand storks were making bricks,
and the curlews with their fellow river birds   1140
brought water from below up to the sky.

Peisetaerus
And who brought clay for them?

First Messenger
                    Herons, in hods.

1126 Elsewhere called a braggart and a weakling.

Peisetaerus
And how'd they got the clay into the hods?

First Messenger
Ah that, my friend, was sheerest genius:
the geese dug into it with their feet like shovels,   1145
and scooped it right into the herons' hods.

Peisetaerus
I guess nothing's impossible if you put your feet to it!

First Messenger
And by god there were the ducks, all wearing belts,
to lay the bricks; and up to join them flew
the swallows with the trowel at their rear, like kiddies,°   1150
and carrying the plaster in their mouths.

Peisetaerus
Then why should anyone continue to hire workmen?
Let's see, what else? Who did the woodwork for
the wall?

First Messenger
          The carpenter birds, a very skilled lot,
were woodpeckers, who pecked out the gates with their beaks;
the din   1155
of their pecking was just like being in a shipyard!
And now those gateways, each and every one,
are gated and bolted and surrounded by guards,
patrolled by bell ringers; and everywhere   1160
the sentries are in place, and signal fires
on the towers. As for me, I'm off to have
a bath; you can finish off the rest yourself.

Chorus Leader
Hey there, what's the matter? Are you really amazed
that the wall's been walled up all so very quickly?   1165

Peisetaerus
My heavens above, I certainly am; and rightly.
To tell the truth, it sounds like a mighty tall tale!
But look, here's a guard coming on the run to report
on events over there, wearing a war-dance look.

Second Messenger
S.O.S! S.O.S! S.O.S!   1170

———————————
1150 The text is obscure and possibly corrupt.

Peisetaerus
What's all this fuss?

Second Messenger
           We're having terrible problems!
Just moments ago a god, one of Zeus' gods,
has flown through the gates and into our airspace,
dodging our daytime sentries, the jackdaws.

Peisetaerus
O dire deed, o deed defiantly done!   1175
Which god?

Second Messenger
        We don't know that; but he had wings,
we know that much.

Peisetaerus
           Then shouldn't you have sent
a patrol in hot pursuit at once?

Second Messenger
          We have:
thirty thousand mounted archer hawks,
and every bird that has hooked talons too,   1180
kestrel, buzzard, vulture, great owl, eagle,
and all the sky's awhirl with the whirring of wings
as that intruding god is hunted down.
And he's not far off; no, he's already somewhere
nearby.

Peisetaerus
        Then shouldn't we be taking up   1185
some slings and arrows? All support personnel
fall in! Shoot and sling! Somebody give me a sling!

Chorus (strophe)
War's broken out,
war beyond words,
between me and the gods!   1190
Now everyone stand guard
on the cloud-girt air,
scion of Erebus,
in case some god
sneaks past you here unseen.   1195

Chorus Leader
And everyone be alert on every side;
the sound of an airborne god's whirring
wings is already audible nearby.

EPISODE

(Iris, Peisetaerus, Chorus)

Peisetaerus
You there! Where where where are you flying? Be still!
Stay right where you are! Halt! Stop that moving!   1200
Who are you? Where from? You better start explaining!

Iris°
From the gods themselves I hail, the Olympian gods.

Peisetaerus
And what's your name? Paralus or Salaminia?°

Iris
I'm Iris the Speedy.

Peisetaerus
            Well, are you boat or bitch?

Iris
What *is* this?

Peisetaerus
          One of you cockerels, fly up there   1205
and grab her!

Iris
         Grab me? What the hell is that
supposed to mean?

Peisetaerus
              You're going to be awfully sorry!

Iris
Well, this is quite extraordinary.

Peisetaerus
                  By what gate
did you pass through the wall, you dirty slut?

Iris
I have absolutely no idea what gate.   1210

1200 Goddess of the rainbow and messenger of Zeus in epic and tragedy, but often rudely
    treated in satyr drama.
1201 See 146 n.

Peisetaerus
Just listen to Miss Innocent up there!
Did you accost our Duty Daws?

Iris
Beg pardon?

Peisetaerus
Did our Storks punch your ticket?

Iris
How dare you!

Peisetaerus
You didn't accept a pass?

Iris
You're sane, I trust?

Peisetaerus
And no Top Cock was around to enter your passage?   1215

Iris
Listen, mister, nobody's entered me at all!

Peisetaerus
And so you just fly in this stealthy way
through a city that's not yours, and through the void?

Iris
But where else are the gods supposed to fly?

Peisetaerus
By Zeus I've no idea, but not through here.   1220
In fact, you're breaking the law right now. Do you realize
that if you got what's coming to you, you would deserve
more than all other Irises to be caught and executed?

Iris
But I'm deathless!

Peisetaerus
You'd be put to death anyway.
Look here, it would be terrible, the way I see it,   1225
if we're to be the rulers but you gods
intend to misbehave and ignore the fact
that it's now *your* turn to obey your superiors.
So tell me now where you're navigating those wings?

Iris
I'll have you know I'm flying from the Father   1230
to mankind with this message: sacrifice

to the Olympian gods; slay sheep on the altars, fill
the streets with their aromas.

Peisetaerus

                          Meaning what?
What gods?

Iris

          I mean us gods, the gods in heaven.

Peisetaerus

So you're gods, eh?

Iris

                     Who else do you think's a god?   1235

Peisetaerus

The birds are gods to humans now, and to them
must humans sacrifice, not, by Zeus, to Zeus!

Iris

Ah fool! Ah fool! Provoke not the terrible
spleen of the gods, lest Justice wielding the Spade
of Zeus eradicate utterly all your race;   1240
lest fiery fumes inflame your body and the embrace
of your palace with thunderbolts Licymnian!°

Peisetaerus

Hey listen, stop your spluttering! Whoa there!
Say, do you think it's a Lydian or a Phrygian
you're trying to give the willies with that kind of talk?   1245
Do you realize that if Zeus annoys me further,
I shall inflame his manse and the halls of Amphion
with flame-throwing eagles,° and furthermore I shall send
up into the sky against him porphyrion
birds dressed up in leopard-skin uniforms,°   1250
more than six hundred strong? Indeed there was a time
when a single Porphyrion caused him plenty of trouble!
And as for you, if you annoy me I'll deal
with the housemaid first: I'll spread her legs and screw her,
with Iris herself in that role; she'll be amazed   1255
how an old hulk like me can stay aloft for three rammings!

1242 According to Schol. "a character in Euripides' *Licymnius* was thunderstruck," but no
    further details are known.
1248 Adapted, according to Schol., from Aeschylus' *Niobe*; cf. also Sophocles *Antigone* 2
    and 1155.
1250 553 n.; some painters thus depicted the Giants.

Iris
Blast you, mister, you and your foul language!

Peisetaerus
Buzz off now, and make it quick! Shoo, shoo! Away!

Iris
I swear my father will put a stop to your insolence!

Peisetaerus
Good grief, why don't you fly away somewhere else,   1260
and give some younger man the hots for you.

Chorus (antistrophe)
We have barred the gods
sprung from Zeus
from any further
passage through my city;   1265
no more shall any mortal
on a single killing floor
send savory smoke to the gods by this route.

EPISODE

(Peisetaerus, First Herald, Xanthias, Manes)

Peisetaerus
It's terribly worrisome, the herald who went
to mankind, if he never comes back again.   1270

First Herald
Hail Peisetaerus, Hail the Blest One, Hail the Most Wise,
Hail the Most Illustrious, Hail the Most Wise, Hail the Most Slick,
Hail the Triple Blest, Hail the—just give me my cue!

Peisetaerus
What's your message?

First Herald
With this crown of gold all the people recognize
and reward you for your wisdom. Here's the crown.   1275

Peisetaerus
I accept. But why do they honor me this way?

First Herald
O founder of the most glorious aethereal city,
don't you realize how greatly you're esteemed among mankind,
and how many you can count as lovers of this land?
Why, before you built this city all men were crazy   1280
for the Spartans: all of them let their hair grow long,

went hungry, never bathed, acted like Socrates,
and brandished batons. But now they've about-faced
and gone bird-crazy, and they're having a wonderful time
imitating birds in everything they do.   1285
For starters, at the crack of dawn they all
fly the coop together, like us, to root for writs;
and then they flock to the archives at city hall
and there they sharpen the bills—they hope to pass.
Why, they're so blatantly bird-crazy that many   1290
even had bird names appended to their own.
There was one lame barkeep by the name of Partridge;°
and then Menippus had the name of Swallow;°
and then Opuntius was the One-Eyed Raven;°
Philocles the Lark;° Theogenes the Sheldrake;°   1295
Lycurgus the Ibis;° Chaerephon the Bat;°
Syracosius the Jay;° and Meidias
was called The Quail, and you know he did look
like a quail who'd been knocked on the head by a hard tapper.°
And from sheer ornithophilia they're all singing   1300
songs that have a swallow in the lyrics,
or that have a duck, or a goose, or maybe a pigeon,
or wings, or even a bit of feather attached.
So much for down below. But I'll tell you one thing:
more than ten thousand of them will be travelling up here,   1305
all desiring wings and a raptor's way of life.
So somewhere you'll have to find wings for the new arrivals.

Peisetaerus
Then we certainly have no time to stand around.
You go as quick as you can and fill the hampers
and all the baskets to the brim with wings,   1310
and have Manes bring the wings out here to me;
I'll stay and greet the visitors as they arrive.

1292 766-68 n.
1293 Unidentifiable.
1294 See 153-4 n.
1295 See 281-2 n.
1295 Unidentifiable.
1296 Son of Lycomedes and grandfather of the homonymous fourth-century statesman;
the nickname implies some connection with Egypt.
1296 The associate of Socrates, often satirized as sallow, thin, and reclusive.
1297 A politician ridiculed for his "barking" oratory and for legislating against comic poets.
1299 Meidias was a public official and avid bird-fighter; in the game of quail-tapping the
bird's handler bet the tapper that his bird would stay in the ring.

DUET
(Chorus, Peisetaerus, Manes)

Chorus (strophe)
Soon some human will be calling
this city very well-manned.

Peisetaerus
Just so our luck holds.   1315

Chorus
Passion for my city grips the world.

Peisetaerus
Faster with those wings, I say!

Chorus
For is anything missing here
that's good for a settler to have?
We've Wisdom, Desire, immortal Graces,   1320
and the happy countenance
of kindhearted Tranquillity.

Peisetaerus
That's pretty lazy service!
Speed it up there!

Chorus (antistrophe)
Quickly, a basket of wings over here;   1325
tell him again to hurry.

Peisetaerus
I will, by hitting him like this!

Chorus
Yes, he's a slowpoke, slow as an ass.

Peisetaerus
A good-for-nothing Manes!

Chorus
But first you must arrange   1330
these wings in proper order:
musical wings here, prophetic there,
and maritime, and then be sure you shrewdly
size up the man when you wing him.

Peisetaerus
By the kestrels I swear you're really for it now;   1335
just look how useless, look how slow you are!

EPISODE
(Father Beater, Peisetaerus, Cinesias, Informer)

Father Beater
O to become a high-flying eagle
and soar beyond the barren pale
over the waves of the gray sea!°

Peisetaerus
That messenger's message looks to be accurate,   1340
for here comes someone singing about eagles.

Father Beater
Hi ho!
There's nothing's quite as much fun as flying! Yes,
I'm bird-crazy, I'm on the wing, I want
to live with you, I yearn for your bird laws.   1345

Peisetaerus
What laws do you mean? The birds have many laws.

Father Beater
All of them! Especially the one where the birds consider
it fine to peck and throttle one's own father!

Peisetaerus
We do in fact consider a bird very manly
who's beaten up his father while still a chick.   1350

Father Beater
That's exactly why I yearn to immigrate here,
to throttle my father and grab for all he has.

Peisetaerus
But we birds have a law, an ancient one
that's written on the Tablets of the Storks:°
"When the father stork has provided for all his storklings   1355
and got them fully fledged, the chicks must then
in their own turn do the providing for their father."

Father Beater
A fat lot of good it's done me coming here,
if I'll even have to *feed* my father now!

Peisetaerus
You won't. Because you came here well disposed,   1360
my lad, I'll fit you with wings like an orphan bird.

1339 From Sophocles' lost play *Oenomaus* (fragment 476).
1354 Recalling the tablets in the Athenian agora on which were inscribed the laws of Draco
    and Solon; one of these concerned mistreatment of parents.

And young man, I'll give you some pretty good advice,
the sort of thing I was taught as a boy myself:
don't beat your father. Instead, take hold of this wing,
and take hold of this spur in your other hand,   1365
and consider this crest your cockscomb. Now off you go:
stand guard! Go on campaign! Work for a living!
Let your father live his life! Since you want to fight,
fly off to the Thracian front and start fighting there!

Father Beater
By Dionysus, that sounds like good advice,   1370
and I'll follow it.

Peisetaerus
                        That's certainly showing sense.

Cinesias°
See, I soar up to Olympus on weightless wings,
I soar now on this path of song,
and now on that—

Peisetaerus
This here's going to take a whole *load* of wings!   1375

Cinesias
with fearless mind and body in quest of a new path.

Peisetaerus
Warm greetings to the twiggy Cinesias!
Why whirl your bandy foot hither in a pirouette?

Cinesias
I wish
to become a bird,   1380
a clear-voiced nightingale.

Peisetaerus
Stop vocalizing, and tell me what you're saying.

Cinesias
I want to get wings from you, then flying up
on high I want to snatch from the clouds preludes
fresh, air-propelled, and swept by scudding snow.   1385

Peisetaerus
You're saying you can snatch preludes from the clouds?

Cinesias
Why, doesn't our whole art depend on them?

1372 A tall, thin composer of dithyrambs in the avant-garde style noted for astrophic
   "preludes," musical complexity, elaborate language, and high emotionalism.

In dithyrambs the dazzling bits are very
airy and dusky and darkly flashing, wing
propelled. Just listen, and you'll soon understand.   1390

Peisetaerus
I'd just as soon not.

Cinesias
                    You absolutely must!
Here, let me run through the whole air for you:
Ah visions of wingéd, sky-coursing
long-necked birds—

Peisetaerus
                    Whoa!

Cinesias
oh to shoot up with a leap   1395
and run with the breaths of the winds—

Peisetaerus
So help me god, I'll put a stop to *your* breaths!

Cinesias
first travelling a southerly course,
then swinging my body northwards,
cleaving a harborless furrow of sky—   1400
That's a very witty trick, old man, and tricky!

Peisetaerus
But I thought that you *enjoy* being wing-propelled!

Cinesias
Is this how you treat me, the director of cyclic choruses,
whose services the tribes always compete for?°

Peisetaerus
Then would you like to stay here with us and serve as director   1405
for Leotrophides,° with a chorus of flying birds,
of the Corncrake Tribe?°

Cinesias
                    It's clear you're mocking me.
But I'll have you know I don't intend to stop,
till I get my wings and scamper through the air!

Informer
Who are these birds, these have-nots   1410

1404 For dithyrambic contests each of the ten Athenian tribes produced its own choruses.
1406 Ridiculed elsewhere as being very thin, like Cinesias.
1406 Punning on the Athenian tribe-name Cecropis.

with dappled wings?
O long-winged iridescent swallow!°

Peisetaerus
This is no small nuisance that's reared its ugly head.
Here comes another one our way, warbling along.

Informer
I repeat: O long-winged iridescent!   1415

Peisetaerus
I think he's singing that song about his cloak;
it's likely to need more than a few swallows!°

Informer
Who is it that issues wings to newcomers?

Peisetaerus
That's me. But you must tell me what you need.

Informer
It's wings I want, wings! Do not ask me twice.°   1420

Peisetaerus
You don't intend to fly straight to Pellene, do you?°

Informer
God no; I'm a subpoena server working the islands,
and an informer—

Peisetaerus
                    What a glorious profession!

Informer
and a lawsuit snoop. So I want to get me some wings
and buzz around the islands serving subpoenas.   1425

Peisetaerus
Subpoena-ing them is more efficient with wingpower?

Informer
God no, it's so the bandits don't hassle me,
and so I can make the return trip with the cranes,
once I've filled up on lots of lawsuits for ballast.

Peisetaerus
So that's your line of work, is it? An ablebodied   1430
young man like yourself informing on foreigners for a living?

1412 Adapted from Alcaeus fragment 345.
1417 Alluding to the proverb "one swallow does not a springtime make."
1420 From Aeschylus' *Myrmidons* (fragment 140), substituting "wings" for "weapons."
1421 A Peloponnesian city where warm cloaks were awarded as prizes in chariot races;
    currently on hostile terms with Athens.

Informer
What else? You see, I don't know how to dig ditches.

Peisetaerus
But surely there are other respectable lines
of work, where a man your size could make an honest
living, instead of cobbling up lawsuits.   1435

Informer
Listen, mister, don't lecture me, just wing me.

Peisetaerus
I'm doing that now, by words alone.

Informer
                                        Just how
can you wing a man with words alone?

Peisetaerus
                                        Why, words
set everyone aflutter.

Informer
                        Everyone?

Peisetaerus
                                        Surely
you've heard boys' fathers talk in the barber shops,   1440
and how they're always saying something like this,
"It's terrible how Dieitrephes talks to my boy
and sets him all aflutter for horse racing!"
Another says his boy's mind's all aflutter
for tragedy, and that it's flown the coop.   1445

Informer
So they actually get wings from words?

Peisetaerus
                                        That's right:
By words is the mind uplifted and a person
transported. That's just how I want to set you
aflutter too: with worthwhile words to convert you
to legitimate work.

Informer
                        But that's not what I want.   1450

Peisetaerus
What *will* you do, then?

Informer
                                I'll not disgrace my family!

Informing's been our livelihood since the time
of my grandfather. Just rig me with the light,
fast wings of a hawk or kestrel, so I can subpoena
the foreigners, then get a judgment here,   1455
then fly back there again.

Peisetaerus
                              I get it now:
you mean the foreigner's case will be lost by default
before he gets here.

Informer
                        That's exactly right.

Peisetaerus
And then while he's sailing here, you're flying back there
to snatch his property.

Informer
                              That's the whole story.   1460
It means whizzing around just like a top.

Peisetaerus
                                    A top—
I know what you mean. And by god I've actually got
some wings here that'll do just perfectly; they're from Corcyra.°

Informer
Good grief, that's a whip you've got!

Peisetaerus
                              No, a pair of wings;
they'll make you whizz around like a top today!   1465

Informer
Good grief!

Peisetaerus
            Why don't you flutter away from here?
Why don't you clear off now, you goddamned pest?
You'll soon get a bitter dose of sleazy shysterism!
Come on, let's gather up these wings and go.

CHORAL INTERLUDE

(strophe)
Many wondrous novelties   1470
have we overflown, and
many amazements have we seen.

1462 Well known for the manufacture of double-thonged whips.

There's a tree, quite exotic,
that grows beyond Wimpdom,
and it's called Cleonymus,°   1475
good for nothing, but otherwise
voluminous and yellow.
Each and every springtime
it sprouts denunciations,
while in wintertime, by contrast,   1480
its shields drop off like leaves.

(antistrophe)
Then there's a far-off country,
at the very edge of darkness
in the lampless steppes,
where people meet the heroes   1485
for lunch and conversation,
except in the evening:
that's when it's no longer
safe to meet them.
For if any mortal happened   1490
to run into the hero Orestes,°
he'd get stripped and paralyzed
all down his righthand side.

EPISODE
(Prometheus, Peisetaerus)

Prometheus
Oh what a fix! Zeus mustn't see me here!
Where's Peisetaerus?

Peisetaerus°
                              Yipes, what could *this* be?   1495
What's all this mufflement?

Prometheus
                              Do you see any gods
back there behind me?

Peisetaerus
                              Can't see nary a one.
But who are *you*?

Prometheus
                              Then what's the time of day?

1475 See 289 n.
1491 See 712 n.
1495 Evidently Peisetaerus has come out to empty a bedpan, cf. line 1552.

Peisetaerus
The time? Well, it's little after midday.
But who are *you*?

Prometheus
                    Is it quitting time, or later?   1500

Peisetaerus
I'm getting damned sick of this!

Prometheus
                    And what's Zeus doing?
Is he clearing the clouds away, or gathering them?

Peisetaerus
Go straight to hell!

Prometheus
                    In that case, I'll get unmuffled.

Peisetaerus
Prometheus, old friend!°

Prometheus
                    Shh, shh! Don't shout!

Peisetaerus
Why, what's up?

Prometheus
                    Shh, be quiet, don't mention my name   1505
You'll be the death of me, if Zeus sees me here.
Look, I'm going to tell you all that's going on
up there, so take this parasol and hold it
over me, so the gods above won't see me.

Peisetaerus
Aha!   1510
That was good thinking, positively Promethean.°
Quick, get under here, and speak without reserve.

Prometheus
Then listen to this.

Peisetaerus
                    Go on, I'm listening.

1502 Prometheus was worshipped at Athens as a fire-god and patron of craftsmen; in
    mythology he took the side of humankind against tyrannical Olympian rule, most
    notably in stealing fire from the gods and giving it to mortals, for which Zeus pun-
    ished him: see Hesiod, *Theogony* 521-616 and Aeschylus' (?) *Prometheus Bound*.
1511 Prometheus' name means "forethought."

Prometheus
Zeus is finished!

Peisetaerus
And just when did this occur?

Prometheus
From the very moment you colonized the air. 1515
Now not a single human sacrifices
to the gods any more, and since that moment
not a whiff of thighbones has wafted up to us;
no, without burnt offerings we're as good as fasting
at the Thesmophoria.° And the barbarian gods 1520
are so hungry that they're shrieking like Illyrians
and threatening to march down against Zeus°
unless he gets the trading posts reopened
so they can import their proper ration of innards.

Peisetaerus
So there are some other gods, barbarians, 1525
up-country from you?

Prometheus
Why shouldn't we have barbarians?
That's where Execestides gets his ancestral god!°

Peisetaerus
And about the name of these barbarian gods,
what might it be?

Prometheus
Their name? Triballians.°

Peisetaerus
I get it;
that must be where "balls to you" comes from. 1530

Prometheus
It's very likely. But I'll tell you one thing for sure:
expect ambassadors about a settlement,
from Zeus and the Triballians up-country.
But don't you ratify a treaty unless
Zeus gives his sceptre back to the birds again 1535
and gives you Princess to be your wedded wife.

1520 An autumn fertility festival celebrated by women alone; on the penultimate day the
     women fasted.
1522 Like an indigenous populace against colonists on the coast.
1527 See 11 n.
1529 A Thracian tribe allied with Athens and noted for their savagery.

Peisetaerus
Who is this Princess?

Prometheus
A very beautiful maiden,
who has custody of Zeus' thunderbolt
and everything else as well: good counsel, law
and order, common decency, shipyards,   1540
mudslinging, paymasters, and three-obol fees.°

Peisetaerus
You mean she looks after everything for him?

Prometheus
That's right: win her from him and you'll have it all.
That's why I came here, to let you in on this.
I've always been a friend to humanity.   1545

Peisetaerus
Yes, if it weren't for you we wouldn't have barbeques.

Prometheus
And I hate all the gods, as well you know.

Peisetaerus
By Zeus, you always were an enemy of the gods,
an absolute Timon.°

Prometheus
I'd better be getting back;
give me my parasol; so even if Zeus does see me   1550
from up there, he'll think I'm attending a basket-bearer.°

Peisetaerus
You may as well carry her stool too; here it is.

CHORAL INTERLUDE

Chorus° (strophe)
Far away by the Shadefoots
lies a swamp, where all unwashed
Socrates conjures spirits.   1555
Pisander° paid a visit there,

1541 The daily pay of a juror, a central civil office exercised by many Athenians on a volunteer basis.
1548 The proverbial Athenian misanthrope.
1551 A maiden chosen for this honor in a religious procession might be accompanied by assistants bearing a parasol and a stool.
1553 This song recalls Odysseus' visit to the underworld as described in *Odyssey* 11 and dramatised in Aeschylus' lost play, *Spirit Conjurers* (*Psychagogoi*).
1556 A general and democratic politician, later turned oligarch; ridiculed elsewhere for cowardice.

asking to see the spirit
that deserted him in life.
For sacrifice he brought a baby
camel and cut its throat,   1560
like Odysseus, then backed off;
and up from below arose to him,
drawn by the camel's gore,
Chaerephon the bat.

EPISODE
(Poseidon, Heracles, Peisetaerus, Triballian)

Poseidon°
This municipality now present to our view   1565
is Cloudcuckooland, the goal of our embassy.
Here, what are you doing, draping your cloak like that,°
from right to left? Please reverse it, this way, to the right.
Oh, you sorry bungler! Are you built like Laespodias?°
Ah democracy, what will you bring us to in the end,   1570
if the gods can elect *this* person ambassador?
Hold still! To hell with you! You're by far the most
barbaric god I've ever laid eyes upon.
Well now, Heracles, what should we do?

Heracles°
                              You've heard
my opinion: I want to choke this guy to death,   1575
whoever he may be, that's blockaded the gods.

Poseidon
Listen, colleague, our charge is to discuss a settlement.

Heracles
All the more reason to strangle him, if you ask me.

Peisetaerus
The cheese grater, someone? Pass the silphium.
And someone get the cheese. Poke up these coals.   1580

Poseidon
Our greetings to you, sir; we're a committee
of three gods.

1564 Brother of Zeus, and thus uncle to Heracles, son of Zeus and the mortal Alcmene.
1567 To the Triballian; Greeks considered the Triballians (now W. Bulgaria) to be barbar-
    ians representing the antithesis of civilization.
1569 A politician, probably elected general shortly before *Birds*, who tried to hide mis-
    shapen calves by draping his cloak very low.
1574 A legendary he-man, worshipped as a hero and god, with a voracious appetite for
    food, drink and sex.

Peisetaerus
                              Wait, I'm grating silphium.
Heracles
  And what sort of meat is that?°
Peisetaerus
                              Some birds who've been
  convicted of attempted rebellion against
  the bird democracy.°
Heracles
                              So that's why you're grating   1585
  silphium on them first?
Peisetaerus
                              Oh, hello, Heracles.
  What's up?
Poseidon
                  We have come as plenipotentiaries
  from the gods, in order to discuss an end to the war.
Peisetaerus
  We don't have any oil in this bottle.
Heracles
  And bird meat should be glistening with it.   1590
Poseidon
  For we gods are gaining nothing by the war;
  while for *your* part, friendly relations with the gods
  would win you ample rainwater for your puddles
  and halcyon days to enjoy all year around.
  On all these issues we're authorized to negotiate.   1595
Peisetaerus
  But it was never *our* side that began hostilities
  against you, and we're ready to make peace now,
  as long as *you're* ready, even at this late hour,
  to do what's right. And what's right amounts to this:
  the sceptre Zeus gives back to us, the birds.   1600
  If we can reach an agreement on these terms,
  I'll be glad to invite the embassy to lunch.
Heracles
  That's good enough for me; I'm voting aye.

1583 Heracles traditionally had an insatiable appetite.
1584 For contemporary Athenian fears about right-wing conspiracies see Thucydides 6.60.

Poseidon
    You what, you damned fool? You idiotic greedyguts!
    You'd rob your father of his rule, would you? 1605

Peisetaerus
    How can you say that? Won't you gods in fact
    have greater power if birds are sovereign down there?
    At present, mortals can hide beneath the clouds,
    and with bowed heads swear false oaths in your names;
    but if you have an alliance with the birds, 1610
    whenever anyone swears "by the Raven and by Zeus,"
    the Raven will happen by and dive-bomb that perjurer
    before he knows it, and peck out his eye like a shot.

Poseidon
    By Poseidon, that's a very good point you make.

Heracles
    I quite agree.

Peisetaerus
            And what do you say?

Triballian God
                        Yeah Bubba. 1615

Heracles
    See? He's in favor too.

Peisetaerus
            Now listen to this,
    something else that we'll do for your benefit.
    If a human vows an offering to a god
    then tries to squirm out of it with a sophism like
    "the gods are patient,"° and out of avarice 1620
    reneges, we'll make him pay up.

Poseidon
              How, pray tell?

Peisetaerus
    When this guy happens to be counting up
    his pennies, or sitting in a nice warm bath,
    a kite will swoop down behind his back and filch
    a two-sheep penalty, and deliver it to the god. 1625

Heracles
    I'm voting aye again, to give them back
    the sceptre.

1620 The full proverb was "the gods are patient, but keep their promises."

Poseidon
>Then ask the Triballian as well.

Heracles
Hey Triballian, how would you like some real pain?

Triballian God
>No
hittum hide wit bat.

Heracles
>He says I'm right.

Poseidon
Well, if that's how *you* both vote, I'll go along.   1630

Heracles
You there: we've voted yes on the sceptre issue.

Peisetaerus
Oh, there's another matter that I just now remember:
the lady Hera I concede to Zeus,
but the maiden Princess must be given to me
as my wife.

Poseidon
>It's not a *settlement* you're hot for!   1635
Let's go back home.

Peisetaerus
>That's of little concern to me.
Cook, please be sure you make the sauce nice and sweet.

Heracles
Man alive, Poseidon, what's your rush, anyway?
Over a single woman we're out to fight a war?

Poseidon
Well, what can we do?

Heracles
>What else? We simply settle.   1640

Poseidon
You chump! Don't you see you've been getting duped all along?
What's more, you're harming yourself. See, if Zeus surrenders
his rule to these birds, you'll be left a pauper when
he dies, because you now stand to get the whole
estate that he leaves behind him at his death.°   1645

1645 Since the Olympian gods were considered immortal, the following scenario would
sound absurd; but at the same time, these gods are now to be replaced.

Peisetaerus
Good grief, how he's trying to give you the runaround!
Come aside here, I want to have a word with you.
Your uncle's out to cheat you, my poor fellow.
Of your father's estate you don't get a single penny;
that's the law.° You see, you're a bastard, illegitimate.   1650

Heracles
A bastard? Me? How's that?

Peisetaerus
                        That's you exactly,
your mother being an alien. Why else do you think
that Athena, as a daughter, could be called The Heiress,
if she had any legitimate brothers?

Heracles
But couldn't my father still leave me his property   1655
as a bastard's portion?

Peisetaerus
                        The law won't let him do that.
Poseidon here, who's getting your hopes up now,
will be the first to dispute your claim to your father's
property, declaring himself to be the legitimate brother.
I'll even quote you the relevant law of Solon:°   1660
    "A bastard shall not qualify as next of kin,
    if there are legitimate children; if there are no
    legitimate children, the next of kin shall share
    the property."   1666

Heracles
You mean I have no share whatever in
my father's property?

Peisetaerus
                        None at all. And tell me,
has your father inducted you into his phratry yet?°

Heracles
Not me he hasn't, and that's always made me wonder.   1670

1650 Throughout this passage, Athenian laws, which granted citizenship only to the children of two Athenian parents, are assumed to apply to the gods; Heracles's mother was a mortal, Alcmene, and already married to Amphitryon.
1660 Solon's codification (early 6th century), to which Athenians tended to attribute all their laws.
1669 A religious guild whose members traced descent from a common ancestor; membership was a standard proof of citizenship, and the induction of young men as new members included lavish feasting.

Peisetaerus
    So why gape at the sky with an assaultive glare,
    when you could side with us? I'll appoint you ruler,
    and promise to supply you with birds' milk.

Heracles
    Your claim to the girl sounds fair to me, as ever;
    And so I'm all for handing her over to you.   1675

Peisetaerus
    And what about you? What do you say?

Poseidon
                                   I vote against.

Peisetaerus
    It's all up to the Triballian. What do *you* say?

Triballian God
    Loverly ya tall missy Princessy
    I hand over birdie.

Heracles
               He says to hand her over.

Poseidon
    No, by Zeus, he's not saying to hand her over;   1680
    if anything, he's just twittering like the swallows.

Heracles
    All right, he's saying hand her over to the swallows.

Poseidon
    Very well, then, you two negotiate the terms
    of a settlement; if that's your decision, I'll keep quiet.

Heracles
    We've decided to agree to all of your proposals.   1685
    Now come with us to heaven yourself, and there
    you'll get your Princess and everything else as well.

Peisetaerus
    Then these birds have been cut up just in time
    for my wedding!

Heracles
             And if you like, I'll stay behind here
    meanwhile, and roast the meat; you go on ahead.   1690

Poseidon
    You? Roasting meat? An orgy of gobbling, you mean.
    Better come with us.

Heracles
> I would have liked that job!

Peisetaerus
Now someone run and fetch me a wedding jacket!

CHORAL INTERLUDE

Over in the land of Extortia, near
the Water Cache,° dwells the wicked   1695
race of Thrive-by-Tongues,
who do their harvesting and sowing
and vintaging by tongue,
and also their culling.
They're a race of barbarians,   1700
Gorgiases and Philippuses.°
It's from these philippic
Thrive-by-Tongues
that all over Attica
the tongue is specially excised.°   1705

Second Herald
You achievers of all success, defying description,
you triple-blessed winged race of birds:
welcome your ruler to his prosperous palace!
Yea he draws near, more dazzling to behold
than any meteor flaring on golden beams,   1710
more even than the flare of the sun's far-beaming
splendor of rays, as he comes escorting a lady
of beauty surpassing description, and brandishing
the thunderbolt, wingéd missile of Zeus.
A fragrance unnamable ascends to the welkin's very   1715
depths, a spectacle fair, and breezes puff
asunder the wreaths of smoke from the fuming incense.
And here he is himself! Now let the divine Muse
open her holy lips in auspicious song!

Chorus
Get back! Divide!   1720
Form up! Make room!
Fly by the man blest with blest luck!
My oh my, her youth, her beauty!
What a blessing for this city

1695 Of fountain houses and also of the device used to time speeches in Athenian lawcourts.
1701 Gorgias, a Sicilian, taught rhetoric at Athens, and Philippus (a common name) was
    either his son or (more likely) a disciple.
1705 I.e., in sacrifices.

is the marriage you have made!   1725

Chorus Leader
Great, great is the luck that embraces
the race of birds
thanks to this man; now with wedding
and bridal songs please welcome
Himself and His Princess!   1730

Chorus (strophe)
Once were Olympian Hera
and the mighty lord of the lofty
throne of the gods
united by the Fates
with such a wedding song.   1735
Hymen Hymenaeus!°
Hymen Hymenaeus!

(antistrophe)
And blooming Eros
of the golden wings guided
the straining reins
as best man at the wedding   1740
of Zeus and thriving Hera.
Hymen Hymenaeus!
Hymen Hymenaeus!

Peisetaerus
I'm pleased by your chants, and pleased by your songs,
and bowled over by your words.

Chorus Leader
Come then, celebrate too   1745
his earth-shaking thunders
and the fiery lightnings of Zeus
and the awesome fulgent thunderbolt.

Chorus
Great golden glare of lightning!
Zeus' immortal firebearing
shaft! Thunders rumbling heavily   1750
in the ground and also bringing rain!
With you this man now shakes the earth,
new master of Zeus' estate
and of Princess, attendant of Zeus' throne.
Hymen Hymenaeus!

1736 The traditional wedding cry.

Chorus Leader

Follow now the wedding party,   1755
all you winged tribes
of fellow songsters, to Zeus' yard
and to the bridal bower.

Peisetaerus

Hold out your hand, my happy one,
and holding to my wings   1760
join me for a dance; I'll
lift you up and swing you!

Chorus

Hip hip hooray! Hail Paeon!
Hail your success, you
highest of divinities!   1765